The Art of Simple Living:
A Guide to Decluttering Your Life

"Transform Your Home in 30 Days"

Mark Tristan Olsson
with
Eleanor Wentworth

The Art of Simple Living: A Guide to Decluttering Your Life

Copyright 2024 © Mark Tristan Olsson with Eleanor Wentworth, The Art of Simple Living: A Guide to Decluttering Your Life

ALL RIGHTS RESERVED

No part of this publication may be reproduced, stored in a retrieval system, or transmitted, in any form or by any means, electronic, mechanical, photocopying, recording, or otherwise, without the author's express written permission.

Disclaimer:

The information provided in this book, "The Art of Simple Living: A Guide to Decluttering Your Life," is for educational and informational purposes only. The content is based on the author's personal experiences, research, and opinions. While every effort has been made to ensure accuracy, the authors and publishers assume no responsibility for errors, omissions, or any consequences resulting from the application of the information presented. Readers are encouraged to use their judgment and consult with professionals where appropriate before making any decisions based on the content of this book. The strategies and suggestions offered are not guaranteed to work for everyone and are intended as general guidance only.

Table of Contents

Dedication 8

About the Authors 9

Chapter 1: 11

The Art of Letting Go: Why Clutter is Like That Ex You Keep Running Into
.... 11

    The Clutter Conundrum: Understanding Emotional Attachment 11

    The Benefits of Decluttering: More Space, Less Stress (and Maybe a Few Extra Snacks) 13

    Digital Decluttering 15

    Eco-Friendly Decluttering 18

    Conclusion 20

Chapter 2: 22

Minimalist Living: Less is More (Except When It Comes to Pizza) 22

    Minimalism 101: A Crash Course for Overachievers 22

    Strategies for Embracing Minimalism: The Joy of Saying No to Stuff .. 26

    The Benefits of Minimalist Living 28

    Long-Term Minimalism: Sustaining a Minimalist Lifestyle 30

    Conclusion 34

Chapter 3: 35

Room-Specific Decluttering: Taming the Beast in Each Room 35

    Bedrooms: Where Clothes Go to Die 35

    Kitchens: The Land of Expired Spices and Mysterious Tupperware 37

    Living Rooms: The Battle of the Remote Controls and Dust Bunnies .. 41

    Emotional and Practical Benefits of Room-Specific Decluttering 45

Conclusion 47

Chapter 4: 49

Decluttering for Families: Kid-Friendly Strategies to Tidy Up (Without Losing Your Mind) 49

    The Great Toy Takeover: How to Regain Control 49

    Involving Kids in the Process: Turning Decluttering into a Game (With Prizes!) 53

    Maintaining a Clutter-Free Home with Kids 55

    The Long-Term Benefits of Decluttering for Families 59

    Conclusion 61

Chapter 5: 62

Digital Decluttering: Because Your Phone Doesn't Need 8,000 Photos of Your Cat 62

    Organizing Your Devices: The Quest for the Holy Grail of Storage 62

    Digital Files: How to Avoid the Black Hole of Unwanted Documents . 66

    The Benefits of Digital Decluttering 68

    Long-Term Strategies for Maintaining a Decluttered Digital Life 72

    Conclusion 73

Chapter 6: 75

Seasonal Decluttering: Tackling Clutter with the Changing Seasons (Goodbye, Winter Coats!) 75

    Spring Cleaning: The Annual Ritual of Dusting Off the Cobwebs 75

    Summer Decluttering: What to Do with All Those Flip-Flops 79

    Autumn Decluttering: Preparing for Cozy and Clutter-Free Spaces 80

    Winter Decluttering: Creating a Warm and Welcoming Home 85

    Conclusion 87

Chapter 7: 88

Stay Passionate 88

The Heart vs. the Home: Finding Balance 88
Creating a Memory Box: Where Sentimental Items Go to Retire 92
Seasonal Decluttering 95
Practical Tips and Encouragements for Emotional Decluttering 97
Conclusion 101

Chapter 8: 103

Eco-Friendly Decluttering: Sustainable Practices for Disposing of Unwanted Items 103

The Three Rs: Reduce, Reuse, Recycle (and Resist the Urge to Hoard) 103
Creative Ways to Donate and Recycle: Giving Your Stuff a Second Life 108
The Benefits of Eco-Friendly Decluttering 111
Long-Term Eco-Friendly Decluttering Habits 113
Conclusion 117

Chapter 9: 118

Time Management for Decluttering: Efficient Schedules and Routines (Because Procrastination is a Real Thing) 118

Setting Realistic Goals: Rome Wasn't Decluttered in a Day 118
Creating a Decluttering Schedule: Making Time for Tidiness 123
Strategies for Efficient Decluttering 125
Long-Term Decluttering Success 130
Conclusion 132

Chapter 10: 134

Decluttering for Seniors: Tailored Approaches for Aging Adults (With a Side of Humor) 134

Understanding Unique Challenges: It's Not Just About the Stuff 134
Tips for Gentle Decluttering: Because Patience is a Virtue 138

5

Strategies for Embracing Minimalism: The Joy of Saying No to Stuff.140

The Benefits of Minimalist Living for Seniors 145

Conclusion 147

Chapter 11: 149

DIY Storage Solutions: Creative Ideas for Organizing Clutter Effectively ...149

Upcycling: Turning Trash into Treasure (or at Least Something Functional) 149

Clever Storage Hacks: Making the Most of Every Nook and Cranny ..151

DIY Storage Solutions for Specific Areas 154

Maintaining Your Clutter-Free Space 159

Conclusion 161

Chapter 12: 162

Conclusion: Embracing a Life of Less (And More Room for Joy) 162

Celebrating Your Decluttering Journey: You Did It! 162

Moving Forward: Living a Life Filled with Purpose and Space 164

Maintaining Your Clutter-Free Space 166

Embracing the Minimalist Mindset 168

Conclusion 171

Chapter 13: 172

The Minimalist Mindset: Cultivating a Life of Intentionality and Joy 172

Understanding the Minimalist Mindset 172

Building Minimalist Habits 174

Minimalism and Relationships 179

Sustaining a Minimalist Lifestyle 181

Conclusion 183

Chapter 14: 185

Minimalist Practices for Everyday Life: Simplify to Thrive 185

    Simplifying Daily Routines 185

    Minimalism in Personal Care and Wellness 187

    Minimalism in Social and Leisure Activities 192

    Sustaining Minimalist Practices 194

    Conclusion 196

Chapter 15: 198

A New Beginning: Living Your Best Minimalist Life 198

    Reflecting on Your Journey 198

    Embracing a Minimalist Future 200

    Celebrating Minimalist Wins 202

    Living a Life of Intentionality and Joy 207

    Conclusion 209

Dedication

"To everyone striving for a simpler, more meaningful life. May this book guide you toward creating space for what truly matters."

About the Authors

"***Mark Tristan Olsson and Eleanor Wentworth*** are inspirational authors, speakers, and life coaches dedicated to helping individuals create a life of simplicity and purpose. With a background in psychology and a deep commitment to personal growth, they have spent over a decade exploring the transformative power of decluttering, both physically and mentally. Raised in homes that valued mindfulness and intentional living, Mark and Eleanor developed a unique perspective on how simplifying one's surroundings can lead to profound inner peace.

They are passionate about helping others declutter their spaces and minds, enabling them to focus on what truly matters. Their compassionate approach and practical wisdom have touched the lives of many, guiding them toward a more fulfilling and balanced life. Known for their engaging storytelling and actionable advice, Mark and Eleanor have become trusted voices in personal development.

They enjoy exploring nature, practicing minimalist living, and volunteering with local sustainability initiatives in their free time. They believe in the power of simplicity to enhance well-being and foster a deep connection to the present moment. Their commitment to helping others achieve a clutter-free, meaningful life is evident in every aspect of their work and personal lives.

"The Art of Simple Living: A Guide to Decluttering Your Life" is a culmination of Mark and Eleanor's experiences, insights, and heartfelt desire to inspire others. Through their writing, they hope to empower readers to embrace simplicity, create space for joy, and live with greater intention."

THE ART OF SIMPLE LIVING: A GUIDE TO DECLUTTERING YOUR LIFE

Mark Tristan Olsson with Eleanor Wentworth

Chapter 1:
The Art of Letting Go: Why Clutter is Like That Ex You Keep Running Into

The Clutter Conundrum: Understanding Emotional Attachment

Introduction to Emotional Attachment

Clutter is the uninvited parasite that is unwelcome in our homes and causes more harm than it brings — it occupies space and increases confusion. But what makes it possible for this experience to continue? The answer can be found in the attitudes that people have towards their belongings, and these are emotional ones. These items are not just objects; they are the physical manifestation of what we have gone through and therefore are sentimental items we do not like to dispose of. It could be a souvenir of an exciting journey, a gift from a dear one, or even an inherited piece from the family; such things merge with our memories and personalities. It is for this reason that one may develop a strong connection to an object making it extremely difficult to let it go even if it may not be very useful. Knowing that such emotions are perfectly healthy and common for many people may be the beginning of the process of unloading clutter. In acknowledging these connections, one can start the process of moving on and making room for now and the next.

Every Item Tells a Story

Every object in our homes means something to us, it can symbolize our history, achievements, and life experiences. A worn-out t-shirt used while on a summer camp may recall positive feelings, just as a forgotten book might remind you of a now-lost friendship. These are not mere things; they are containers of memories, the feelings and values of the time that has been experienced. Whether you collected in some foreign country that painting you have hung on the wall or the old guitar you do not play anymore each of them is a page in the book of your life. Addressing such attachments is part of the way that decluttering has to be approached. This is not the same as ignoring the memories but rather one has to accept them and then see what must be preserved. What I am getting at is this process of confronting and deciding aids in producing clarity, in the physical sense within our homes and workspaces, and mentally within our cognition. In choosing what to retain and what to let go, we keep a part of our history and open doors to the future.

Dealing with Sentimental Items

Sorting through our stuff can be like sifting through a soupy mess of memory where it is critical to figure out whether you have joyful items or dusty relics. An object that was the source of joy may now only be a constant symbol of the good times that are no longer present. In this, one can retain the memory without the physical mess. Among the effective methods is to consider making photographs of 'valuable' things; this way, the given object will be captured and separated to leave no physical reminder of the memory. The beauty of digital storage is that such memories can remain preserved in such an archive without occupying the physical space within one's home. This approach enables one to retain the value of an item while at the same time, extending maximal restraint towards the space that pervades their surroundings. That's why it is possible to speak not only about respecting memories and ideas but also about the creation of a more comfortable and organized environment. Also, it is possible to make separate albums of such memories as a digital scrapbook or memory album, which will also help preserve such memories and not clutter up the physical space.

Clutter in Families

Clutter is not a phenomenon that affects a single person; it is characteristic of families and residential spaces where everyone brings things in. Members of a household have different degrees of affection toward things and this makes it hard to deal with clutter at home. Due to this, there is a need to involve the entire family in the process of deleting their unsuitable items. It is especially useful to involve children in cleaning — by making tidying up the bonus play, you will foster in them the basic principles of tidiness and frugality. Make use of games or challenges where by completing them one earns points that can be exchanged for the required items. It not only makes the home to be tidy but also brings about family unity in the process of putting arrangements in place. When decluttering becomes a family affair it trains the entire family to be aware of clutter and to be intentional in getting rid of it. It is also advisable to come up with a working system of free and open discussion about which things are important and why in this case omniscience and a variety of perceptions can also be useful to brainstorm why clutter is undesirable for both partners and to work out the ways of clutter-free and cheerful living together.

The Benefits of Decluttering: More Space, Less Stress (and Maybe a Few Extra Snacks)

Mental Clarity

Both physically and psychologically, de-cluttering is more than just organizing; it helps in eliminating clutter. The lack of clutter automatically results in decreased stress and anxiety levels because the surroundings are orderly and balanced. If everything has a home, the mind is not bogged down with a sense of urgency on clutter, which in turn gives you that great sense of relief as you clear up your mind for greater clarity of thought. This leads to improved concentration since your mind can easily avoid distractions occasioned by clutters. Fewer items result in less confusion and hence, everyday operations are made easier and less time-consuming. Just think about waking up in a clean house where there are no problems of searching for something in the mountains of things. By decluttering, one prepares the environment for a less cluttered and therefore more productive, less stressful mentally and energy-wise life where mind and effort goes where it is entitled.

Emotional Well-Being

Not only does decluttering involve the removal of physical items, but it has emotional repercussions as well. Sometimes, ridding oneself of items that do have not much use can be very liberating since the items that you let go of may be full of memories and could bring you down. What I have been noticing is that as you take away all the hindrances, literally and metaphorically, you make room for more of what counts. This shift enables you to focus on the things that matter — meaningful relationships with people and efficient time-spending on activities that are meaningful for you. This is so because adopting the habit of keeping space, your furniture, your belongings, and your life free from clutter is an advocacy for change since clutter breeds stagnancy. Decluttering is not just the process of throwing things away; decluttering is about the creation of space for happiness, enough, and what matters.

Physical Health

A clean home is not only desirable to the eye; it is an essential part of maintaining physical health. This is because the clutter you create adds to the number of things that you have to clean and hence when these things are removed, cleaning is much easier. This means it will be easier for you to keep your home clean and this is a direct boost to your health. The kind of environment created means that there are few surfaces for dust, pet dander, and other pollutants to adhere to and thus, greatly decreases incidences of respiratory illnesses, etc. Such a hygienic and neat environment is ideal for an individual to feel relieved and even be healthy. You'll breathe easier—physically and metaphorically—knowing that your home environment is healthy and clean and enhancing your body's health in every aspect.

Improved Relationships

Clutter is disruptive in shared areas of a house, and when things get lost it leads to disagreements between family members. Decluttering brings about organized environments that do not cause discomfort hence people will be less inclined to disagreements. An organized home is calm and people work together as they are aware of the things that are expected to be placed where and anyone looking for anything will quickly locate it. Such mutual rage created given tidiness may enhance the family bond and make it a united front against clutter, and therefore, turn cleaning into a family activity. Whether one is engaged in side-by-side management to sort through the mess or come home to find that the space has been tidied, thus bringing calm, then it blossoms relations and strengthens home togetherness.

Digital Decluttering

Introduction to Digital Clutter

Even in today's world of virtual mess, clutter is not just limited to the four corners of the house. Through our devices, be it a phone, tablet, or computer, we have numerous files, apps, and notifications piling up and making our screens cluttered. As if your room is full of someone else's stuff that you have to sort out, so is this digital clutter that can stress and ultimately decrease your production. Every day when you turn on your device, there are hundreds of options; it takes its toll in terms of cognition and affect. However, they found that a clean digital environment is advantageous in several ways. No more need to lose your thoughts and become overwhelmed and unfocused by an uncontrolled digital environment – it's time to take back your mind and streamline your productivity. Clearing all the noise and clutter out of a digital life not only helps to save time but also implodes a new form of happiness that would have been impossible to achieve through the constant bombardment of useless information.

Steps to Digital Decluttering

The first process of digital decluttering involves sorting your files, directories, and subdirectories or directories and subdirectories. An organized system of various documents, photos, or other files in their folders should be organized and given clear names. This makes certain items easier to find than skating through piles of clutter that may overwhelm students daily. Next, deal with the unwanted apps as well as files that are just occupying the space on your device for no reason. Therefore, from time to time, users should go through the applications on the device and remove the ones that are not essential in the current context, and files that are copied or outdated. Organizing and storing photos and videos is another aspect—go through your photo and video galleries and delete unnecessary screenshots or anything that doesn't contain a memory of value or utility, for example. This way, you declutter your digital content and your device will run fast and anything you do will be faster and easier to accomplish.

Maintaining a Clutter-Free Digital Space

Clutter freedom in one's digital environment means having to start afresh from time to time after which a person has to get out of their comfort zone to ensure that the unwanted is removed – it is however a worthy venture. First things first: set yourself up for digital spring cleaning, for example, weekly or monthly check-ins during which you go through your files and applications. Create order out of the chaos and make it a point that each new file and each new app has its place. By keeping to this method in the future, there will be no build-up of clutter and the control of your digital life becomes relatively simple. However, to lesser distractions, switch off unnecessary notifications and use fewer applications within the current day/week. Decluttering the device usage not only frees a man from active use of multiple devices but also from time to time allows him to focus on what is important in life and also makes one work much more effectively.

Embracing Digital Minimalism

Digital minimalism is all about what is meaningful in one's digital life, decluttering, and ensuring that technology is serving you rather than the other way around. The first step is to find out which of the applications or tools you have been using enhances your life. It is crucial to focus on these necessities and, at the same time, free oneself of anything not necessary. This approach helps eliminate the measures that can cause drastic interruption of the digital environment and effectiveness. By practicing digital minimalism, you create an optimal context where you spend time on purpose, and the presence of digital distractions is reduced as a general rule. What it leads to is a much less cluttered digital environment that is also one that fits more in line with your values and constraints.

Eco-Friendly Decluttering

Sustainable Practices

Decluttering can be done sustainably without leading to more waste in the environment. When donating and recycling items you will be able to take a product, but instead of throwing it away, you will be able to give it a new life. If clothes no longer fit, instead of throwing them away, they should be donated to various charity organizations to whoever may need them. Another way of making sure that any given material such as paper, glass, or electronics is dealt with in an environmentally friendly manner is through recycling. Upcycling and repurposing provide far more innovative approaches to solving the same problem. Renovate previous objects to provide them with new functions, for example, transform a ladder into a bookcase or use glass jars as jugs. This not only helps in cutting the expenses of buying new items for the rooms but also makes it feel like it is yours. As was pointed out earlier, the objective is to reduce what is being trashed as much as possible. It is helpful to find new homes for the products so that they stay useful; thus, it can achieve successful cluttering in an eco-friendly manner.

Creative Decluttering

Decluttering isn't necessarily a boring chore; it can be an outing. Repurposing is a wonderful thing for any home since it involves turning old items into new pieces that can be useful. For example, an old wooden crate can be repurposed into a side table to give your interior an authentic vibe, or a stack of old magazines can be made into an art piece to hang on a wall: DIY projects will help you get rid of clutter making your items not only functional but also beautiful. However, these projects also help make waste minimal and can let your creativity shine. Decluttering is not just about cleaning up or arranging; it is a space to start thinking creatively about what can be achieved with objects.

This means that if you approach decluttering creatively, what once would have been considered trash can become something cherished, a unique item.

Community Involvement

Decluttering can extend beyond your home and benefit your entire community. Donating usable items to local charities is a simple yet impactful way to support those in need while reducing waste. Many organizations are in constant need of clothing, household goods, and other items that you may no longer need. Another effective way to involve the community is by organizing or participating in garage sales. These events not only help you declutter but also create opportunities for neighbors to find value in items you no longer use. Additionally, consider starting a sharing or swapping initiative in your community. By exchanging items, you promote sustainability and reduce the need for new purchases, which in turn helps the environment. Through these community-driven efforts, your decluttering process becomes a shared journey toward a more sustainable and connected way of living.

Long-Term Benefits

Decluttering is not only limited to your home but can positively impact your community as well. Giving away items that are still in usable condition to charities in your area is another method of helping the community while also recycling. Most organizations are always in need of clothes, household items as well as other items you may wish to donate. To get the community's cooperation, another method proven to be quite fruitful is through the use of garage sales, either by the social workers themselves or by arranging for such sales. These events not only support people in tidying up their unwanted items but also provide a chance for neighbors to benefit from things that are no longer used by owners. Also, one may consider beginning the sharing or swapping program in your locality. Swapping eliminates the use of resources in having to buy new products, which is beneficial to the environment. In this manner, the process of decluttering becomes a social and community-based process of constructing a more environmentally friendly and socially integrated lifestyle.

Conclusion

Recap of Benefits

Organizing provides for many positive feelings and practical values. The feeling and movement aspects of it enable you to cast off something that wasn't serving you, and therefore provide a sensation of liberation and decreased pressure. It also enables the clearing of the mind and enables one to leave what is trivial and concentrate on what is meaningful. In practice, decluttering means a less tiring, easier-to-clean and maintain home, free of unnecessary distractions. It adds free time to the things that one enjoys, making life a richer experience. With removal, you create space for harmony and tidiness in your setting and that is likely to enhance your health and your interpersonal affairs.

Embracing the Process

I believe that decluttering is a process and not a one-time event where you just clean up and it's done. Take it lightly and kindly for yourself and others with the realization that it is alright to go step by step. Smile at the highs and lows and be gentle to yourself when you discard what does not benefit you anymore. The facts are still facts and therefore no matter how small an advancement is, it is an advancement nonetheless. When you declutter trying to look at the process in a positive light, you will discover that it is something that can be easily accomplished but brings much satisfaction.

Looking Forward

Looking ahead, get positively charged for new experiences that a clutter-free life is going to offer you. When your room has no clutter, you feel the potential to do things you never used to do, hang out with loved ones, and foremost, the feeling of living in a clean environment. The journey of decluttering leaves one to live the desired life which is genuine and surrounded with belongings that could give meaning.

Chapter 2:
Minimalist Living: Less is More (Except When It Comes to Pizza)

Minimalism 101: A Crash Course for Overachievers

Introduction to Minimalism

Minimalism can be described as a monastic or a hipster thing that few people need, while it is an option for everybody who wants to have a stress-free and efficient life, especially for hard-working people. People used to believe that minimalism is the act of leaving behind all things one has an interest in. But it is not about controlling your life and deciding what can or cannot be allowed into it; rather, it is about choosing within the constraints of reality what has any worth. Minimalism is the process of removing unnecessary elements from our lives, and it should be used as a weapon against cluttering, to help people reach their goals. By getting rid of anything excessive, minimalism helps you to give your focus to your goals much easier. While striving for more, and being more austere at the same time is not about getting rid of the things that hold your valued possessions; it is about making decisions on what remains important to you. This approach enables you to declutter your environment while being able to keep and contain items that give you joy or fit your goals and dreams.

The Art of Decluttering Your Home

If you need to declutter your home, the first thing you notice can be extremely tiring, but if you begin with minor things, you will see that you can certainly manage this. Start with the single room, and commit to working for exactly 20 minutes – during which time, sort any items you find into "keep", "donate", and "recycle" piles. This way we do not get bored and don't feel overwhelmed, and at the same time we gradually accumulate the results needed every step of the way. In the bedroom: declutter – remove those things that you have been keeping 'just in case' When designing a bedroom, get rid of clothes that are not used, and those gadgets that only contribute to increasing the clutter. At home get into the kitchen sort out the junk drawer and get rid of extra utensils that are of the same kind. Decluttering your living room means that you have to take back the space from objects that do not need to be in the room and find order for the ones that stay. The idea here is to get each room exactly right; to turn each into the efficient and uncluttered sanctuary that you require to be able to effectively process thoughts without becoming overwhelmed.

Kid-Friendly Decluttering

Teaching and informing loved ones, especially children about the process of the decluttering process can be enjoyable. I learned that whenever possible it is best to make cleaning processes a sort of game for kids so that they do not see it as a task that has to be done but as a fun mission. For example, you can set up a scavenger hunt in which kids look for items that will be donated or disposed of properly and after they are done, you reward them appropriately. Schedules are the most important means of preventing clutter from invading the living space. Engage the youngsters in the tidiness activities such as the packing of toys before going to bed to check on the habit formation. To make the process engaging ensure that children are given points or stickers for getting engaged in the de-cluttering process. These points can be exchanged with a treat or a fun activity. By using games for decluttering you educate your kids on the importance of order, and responsibility, and how it is beneficial to live in a clean environment at home.

Digital Decluttering

Digital clutter is as bad as the physical one, and it silently fills the empty shelves until it becomes a problem. Here, the first step towards organizing digital environments is to identify how the various applications interfere with attention and performance. Frequent clean-ups are vital; perhaps one can set a date when he or she has to conduct a 'monthly cleanup' of files, applications among other things, and photos. It does not have to take hours—the rubdowns can be done in half an hour and the effects are always felt. It is also good to declutter during the different seasons of the year. As much as you should consider cleaning up your home when the seasons change, it is also important to 'spring clean' your life online. This involves reviewing the email subscriptions one has, categorizing the files that are on the desktop, and deleting the documents that are not pertinent to the current activities. This way by maintaining the general cleanliness of virtual spaces one eliminates unnecessary noises, improves the rates of work, goes through less stress, and brings into the mind only those things that are necessary.

Day 1:
Reflect on Why You Want to Declutter

Questions to Consider	Check
Do I like it?	[ ]
Is it just plain ugly?	[ ]
Does it have a funny smell I can't get rid of?	[ ]
Do I like the color?	[ ]
Does the texture feel nice?	[ ]
Is it 2 sizes away from fitting me?	[ ]
Have I used it in the past 3 years?	[ ]
Have I opened it recently?	[ ]
Is it associated with bad memories?	[ ]
Does it make me feel guilty?	[ ]
Is it something I bought on impulse?	[ ]
Does it take up more space than it's worth?	[ ]
Is it still functional or just taking up space?	[ ]
Does it align with the life I want to live?	[ ]

Why Am I Keeping It?	Check
Am I just keeping it because someone gave it to me?	[ ]
Am I keeping it in the hope it will have value one day?	[ ]
Is it part of something else I lost a long time ago?	[ ]
Have I got more than one of them?	[ ]
Do I need that many?	[ ]
Is it cheap and easy to replace?	[ ]
Does it serve a current purpose in my life?	[ ]
Am I holding onto it out of obligation or guilt?	[ ]
Does it reflect who I am today or who I was?	[ ]
Would I buy it again today if I didn't already own it?	[ ]

Action	Check
Write down your reasons for decluttering.	[ ]
Visualize the benefits of a clutter-free space.	[ ]
Set a specific intention for what you hope to achieve.	[ ]
Identify any emotions tied to your belongings.	[ ]

Strategies for Embracing Minimalism: The Joy of Saying No to Stuff

Handling Free Stuff

Promotional products that you receive free of charge are equally a nuisance if they do not have an actual use. To learn how to be minimalist, begin with assessing the relevance of such incentives: Self-reflecting, considering whether the particular item is beneficial and necessary in one's life or serves as mere clutter. They might be the things one uses in a moment of excitement and later feels the items are just left to gather dust in a drawer. Start declining things that do not bring joy or have utility. In doing so you not only save yourself from a future bout of clutter but also train yourself into a more quality-centric mentality. Well, just as a reminder, it's perfectly acceptable not to take free stuff—it's a tiny move toward having no clutter in one's dwelling. The act of embracing less means paying attention to what you let into your home and making sure it represents the kind of life you wish to live.

Dealing with Emotional Clutter

This type of clutter is as stressful as the physical one, but there are ways how to cope with it. The initial and perhaps one of the most helpful ones is the concept of a so-called "Maybe Later" box. This enables you to keep special items that you do not wish to discard yet, but that you can revisit after some time when you apply a new perception. Long-term periodicity is crucial – it is useful to decide on fixed dates when the importance of these objects will be re-evaluated. Meanwhile, the service rendered to own items dwindles, and other contingencies assert themselves, rendering it easier to make a change. It goes hand in hand with driving the improvement in the amount of emotional clutter and generates clarity and tranquillity. Thus, when you start releasing things that don't have personal meaning to you anymore, practically all of which give you a string of memories to hold on to and keep you anchored to the present – you sever those links and start fresh. Thus, this type of minimalism promotes self-development and provides a better way of interacting with items chosen for one's possession.

Family Decluttering Strategies

It is easy for children to get bored but making a decluttering process a kind of game is creative so you turn this boring process with your family into enjoyment. Another fun way to go about it is to involve the kids and make decluttering a fun hunt for the kids. The idea was to set a challenge for them to look for things that they do not need anymore or have not used for a long time and then choose what to do with those items, whether to donate them or not. It is also fun, which makes it functional, and educative to the children on aspects of generosity and the essence of simple living. Also, it can be useful to apply decluttering as a nice time to spend with children. Explain the benefits for people who practice minimalism and the benefits of having a clean space. By doing so, it gives the signal that the practice of minimalism is something that the whole family is going to achieve together. It's important, that these activities teach children to be responsible, and to understand the advantages of a non-cluttered life so that decluttering is not an ordeal but a good family habit.

Digital Decluttering Strategies

Digital clutter is something that can distract you just as physical clutter can, thus it is necessary to have clean-up sessions at least once a week. Begin with ensuring that there are special days when you can unplug and purge your email inbox and desktop and other folders you use as well as unnecessary applications. This assists in liberating space on the digital sets and facilitates the efficient performance of the devices. The underlying trend is to declutter your digital life: there is no need to have several applications or tools you do not need for productivity purposes. In this way, by filtering the noise, one creates more of a deliberate and meaningful experience online. The benefits you derive from this strategy are not only enhanced organization but also enhanced cognition. An efficient digital space can greatly improve your quality of presence by letting you focus on what is the most important in your private or business life. To invest in less online – or rather, in fewer online distractions – means moving closer to embracing digital minimalism as an approach to life.

The Benefits of Minimalist Living

Mental Clarity

The first and probably the most apparent effect of minimalism is that it clears the mind. It is self-explanatory that a clean and uncluttered space can bring a fair degree of calm and lessen anxiety levels because there is nothing to get in the way. If you manage your surroundings well, it becomes much easier to just do what you do: work, play, live, contemplate. The absence of clutter also results in mental clearing so you can focus and work better. You also do not get distracted by the numerous reminders of things that have not been completed or the clutter around you hence your mind can rest thus enabling you to make sound decisions. This headspace is not just a lack of stress; it is about having an environment within which you can be at your best – able to think more effectively and to live in a way that is more deliberate and purposeful.

Emotional Well-Being

Living with less has a very meaningful effect on an individual's psychological state. At the same time with material things, there are feelings, memories, and emotions tied to them, all of which disappear when the things are cleared away. This process liberates the heart and the psychological self as one frees oneself from the burden of dealing with the clutter of the past. Living a minimalist life means that it is easier for you to leave life with no regrets; you chase what makes you happy and content in life. Opposing complexity, an environment that is simple steers clear of greed and fosters satisfaction that allows people to value genuine needs in life. Elimination of the excess also implies that there are fewer things to divert your attention and that you live a more engaged life in the present. There is a feeling of in-tune living here, and, it's intentional, which in turn can lead to a state of profound happiness and emotional well-being.

Physical Health

Minimalism also has tangible advantages in that it ensures one has a clean house and it is beneficial to our health. Since there will be less mess around, the living areas stay relatively easy to dust and sweep, and this in turn frees up your time and energy to arrange your home as you like. It also helps improve physical health since you are sure the environment surrounding you is clean, and it lowers allergens and the quality of air. An organized space reduces the chances of dust and mold build-up and other allergens that are bad for your health. Also, when a home is well arranged and well planned, there is a reduction in the chances of an accident or an injury. When you stick to minimalism, you achieve a home infrastructure that fosters your health and comfort, making it simpler to practice physical health.

Improved Relationships

Minimalist living can greatly enhance your relationships by creating a more harmonious home environment. A clutter-free space reduces the potential for conflicts that often arise from disorganization or misplaced items. When everyone knows where things belong and the home is easy to maintain, there's less stress and more time to enjoy each other's company. This shared sense of order fosters a peaceful atmosphere where positive interactions can thrive. Additionally, with less time spent managing clutter, you can focus more on meaningful interactions with your loved ones. Minimalism encourages quality time together, whether it's enjoying a meal without the distraction of clutter or simply relaxing in a serene, organized space. By simplifying your surroundings, you create a home that supports stronger, more fulfilling relationships, allowing you to connect more deeply with those who matter most.

Long-Term Minimalism: Sustaining a Minimalist Lifestyle

Eco-Friendly Decluttering

The essence of living a minimalist life pertains to environmentally friendly ways of decluttering. Donating, Recycling or even upcycling products means contributing to the decrease of waste products hence preserving the environment. What this means is that your decluttering projects will be a plus to your life, and the life of the planet. This way, people get valuable use out of the items, that they might require, and at the same time, you get to spare space in your house. Recycling properly enables the papers, plastics, or electronics to be given back to the circulation to be used again therefore minimizing the number of raw materials that must be produced, and hence minimizing the emission of greenhouse gases. Recycling is a creative aspect that ensures that the process of getting rid of clutter comprises the aspect of creativity. Recycling means giving a new look to the items that otherwise are of no use – for instance, instead of throwing away an old ladder, you build a bookshelf out of it or repurpose glass jars as storage containers, which serve the purpose of the minimalist adage of utilizing what is available to the optimum.

Maintaining Minimalism

Living a minimalist life is not an easy thing and one must continue practicing the necessary things in everyday life. The last thing to do is build up those habits that will help you to de-clutter and stop this process as soon as you start to see signs of it. It is pertinent to note that some of the consistent, simple tasks like spending 10 minutes daily to pick things and put them in order can go a long way in preventing clutter. This can be done through certain daily activities that make them aware of their surroundings and therefore can make minimalism a subconscious way of their lives. Also, it is necessary to perform periodic 'seasonal clean-outs' to keep up the minimalist lifestyle for the long haul. When the season changes, it is a good time you review some of the items that you may have and let go of the ones that are not useful. This helps you to always put your current needs into practice hence ensuring that the environment around you is always on with your minimalistic standards. Seasonal reviews also prove effective as they allow change to be effected as it will be seen that even the best of homes require change now and then especially to ensure that the home meets the occupant's needs.

Mindful Consumption

Being careful when purchasing items to use is one of the pillars that can help support minimalist lifestyles sustainably. Intentional consumption is all about not allowing anything into your life by accident; every choice is deliberate, and every object has a purpose. It also avoids the overcrowding of a subject's space by their possessions and guarantees that one's environment is not congested. To avoid this, consider setting measures like not purchasing without thinking about it for at least 24 hours or if the item adds value to your life. Such practices discourage impulsive purchasing and thus minimize the chances of making purchases that will form clutter. At some point, mindfulness is incorporated into your daily life and you learn how to make the right choices that are consistent with minimalism. Availing yourself to only a few things encourages you to surround yourself with objects of value, thereby backing up minimalist principles while at the same time improving your way of life.

Embracing the Minimalist Mindset

The concept of minimalism is far from just throwing away things and ridding oneself of material things – it's about being content with less. The joy of less comes from the freedom to focus on what truly matters: a fulfilling, meaningful, and enriching pattern of education focusing on the growth and development of the individual as well as meaningful interactions with peers and faculty. It will be seen that when all our concern is taken up with the things that money can buy, there is no room for anything more worthwhile. This mindset helps you to direct your time and effort to the right activities that positively endow you with joy and do not exhaust you with a burden accomplished by just heaping up on material things. What this does is that you dedicate yourself to the most important things in life and thus create a purposeful life. As you live with fewer items, you can feel the liberty and serenity that comes with a clean environment which consequently makes life full of meaning and happiness.

Day 2:
Research the Psychological Impact of Clutter

Questions to Explore	Check
How does clutter affect my mental clarity?	[ ]
What is the emotional toll of living in a cluttered space?	[ ]
How does clutter impact my productivity and focus?	[ ]
Does clutter increase my stress or anxiety levels?	[ ]
How does a cluttered space affect my relationships?	[ ]
What are the long-term effects of living in a cluttered environment?	[ ]
How does clutter influence my decision-making abilities?	[ ]
Can clutter contribute to feelings of overwhelm?	[ ]

Research Ideas	Check
Read articles on the psychological effects of clutter.	[ ]
Watch videos or TED talks on minimalism and well-being.	[ ]
Consult experts or read books on the impact of clutter.	[ ]
Explore studies on how clutter affects brain function.	[ ]
Look into the connection between clutter and physical health.	[ ]
Research the link between clutter and decision fatigue.	[ ]

Action	Check
Use this knowledge to motivate yourself.	[ ]
Write a summary of what you learned.	[ ]
Reflect on how this research impacts your motivation to declutter.	[ ]
Share your insights with someone else to solidify your understanding.	[ ]

Conclusion

Recap of Minimalism Benefits: Essentials of minimalism extend far and wide reaching every facet of life, with numerous advantages to embrace. On the mental level, it helps to improve the decision-making process since there are fewer distractions to distract one from that which is most important. Mentally, minimalism fosters stillness and satisfaction because removing more anxiety-provoking objects ensures fewer worries. Tangibly, the minimalism entails non-accumulation of many belongings reducing the chances of clutter and making many places look neat and conducive for working. Compared to materialism, it promotes the value of genuine relationships and important events, as people focus on partners and events rather than things.

Embracing the Lifestyle: When you are going for the minimalist lifestyle, do so with fun, art, and passion. I want to stress, however, that it is not about exclusion because the key idea is driven by the definitions a person makes intentionally. While embarking on the journey, be free-spirited and do not stress yourself while looking for what minimalism is all about to you. Try hard to make your life easier and less full of unnecessary things – from furniture and clothes to deadlines and meetings. Lastly, focus more on the process than on the result as the process will indicate that minimalism is a journey.

Looking Forward: The prospects that are opening in front of the person in terms of becoming a new person in minimalism are unlimited. In so doing you are not just doing away with clutter from your home, but making your life happier, more organized, and more fulfilling. Minimalism shows a real possibility of having quality in life and being able to do what one enjoys and avoid what triggers frustration. Moving further into the practice of minimalism, life becomes less cluttered and chaotic but at the same time, it becomes more meaningful with more attention to the people who matter.

Chapter 3: Room-Specific Decluttering: Taming the Beast in Each Room

Bedrooms: Where Clothes Go to Die

Introduction to Bedroom Decluttering

The bedroom is one of the most interesting rooms in the house: it is a place to rest and, at the same time, a storage area. Organized as a zone of rest and dreaming, it can quickly turn into a storage for clothes and other things. For example, clothing especially if worn has a unique way of collecting and transforming this serene place into a full-blown storage. Heaps of unused clothes, other accessories such as unpolished shoes for years, and socks that do not correspond in color soon transform the organizer's area into a mess. For your bedroom to be a restful sanctuary as it should be, then the clutter has to go – and order restored. Apart from making the surrounding ambiance more pleasant, this contributes to the formation of the conditions that allow having a better night's rest and, therefore, a better start in the morning.

Confronting the Chaos

If you have been struggling to define order from the mess that is in the bedroom, then you should not worry. First, disregard your garments as rowdy revelers who misread the host's tired signals and wish to make a meal out of it and bolt. Get ready for the work with a sense of humor and a clearly defined strategy. Set a timer for 20 minutes and focus on sorting your items into three categories: proprietary are to keep, donate, and recycle. It also makes the work more urgent and does not let you engage overly with the seemingly minor details of the strategy. If you do not want to get confused, begin with a single room or part of your room, for instance, a wardrobe. It is easier to commit to a series of small tasks than a single large one – by doing it this way you will find it much easier to build up the energy and motivation needed to make a change with your tidiness levels.

The "Try It On" Challenge

The "Try It On" challenge is one of the best ways to determine what should remain in your home and what should not. Get your bed to transform into a fashion runway and wear and model every outfit that you have. Now is the time to decide if it does fit, look good, and make you feel glamorous in any way. If an item of clothing does not conform to the above requirements, the only thing to do is to bid it farewell and put it in a donation bin. Entice yourself during this process – it is not healthy to hold on to clothes that you haven't worn for years. They suggest one should fail to keep only the clothes they feel a sort of affinity for or those they will use more often. This challenge not only makes your place tidy and sleek but also makes sure that you have appropriate clothes that you like to wear.

Emotional Attachments

Most people have a hard time throwing away clothes and this mainly comes as a result of the sentimental value that is associated with them. To some extent, it is necessary to admit the emotional attachment of a person to the given item and at the same time to understand that there is no need to consider this thing vital to keep it. A useful idea is to make photographs of the things that are dear to you before parting with them. This helps you to retain the memory in the absence of occupying space. While disposing of your items, it is good to do so with the thought in mind that the space created is for new experiences and memories. This sort of mentality change can help reduce the defeatist mentality that comes with decluttering and more towards a creation process. Finally, cleaning up a bedroom is a way of taking care of the self, as you are merely arranging your surroundings for personal growth.

Kitchens: The Land of Expired Spices and Mysterious Tupperware

Introduction to Kitchen Decluttering

The kitchen can easily turn into a sensual, warm, place of creative culinary miracles. But it can look more like one of those unfortunate kitchen accidents where spices and splashes of food are covered with dust. There is a simple mantra that one has to follow to redesign the kitchen: less is more. Consider first how you can open with the fact that most people have random and expired spices and condiments lurking in the back of their pantry. Not only do such items occupy a lot of space, but their use is also related to the quality of the final dish. The removal of the products that have expired, will make your kitchen look fresh and operational all the time. Cleaning your kitchen doesn't only entail making it have a neat look but it involves optimizing the space for use in cooking or baking. The idea of getting rid of the clutter means that your kitchen will become more utilization-friendly, efficient, and a pleasure to transform into the soul of your home.

Taming the Tupperware Monster

Tupperware – while a handy tool – does not always remain systematically owned with the variety of lids and containers scattered. Taming this monster begins with a simple sort: return a lid to the store and the identical container, and dispose of those which cannot have an association. It will immediately minimize the amount of stuff in your kitchen cabinets. The best course is to practice essentialism—now you can only use the containers that are necessary for the given period and the ones you use daily. Acquiring furniture like stackable containers in a single set can also simplify how property is arranged and organized, and aesthetically. This not only helps in sparing space but also makes cooking and storing food easier and more efficient. The above methods of sorting your Tupperware ensure that the exercise of looking for the individual components is done away with and your kitchen is much more ordered and efficient. Consequently, the goal is to keep the environment as clean as possible without having it impede one's cooking.

Dealing with Expired Spices

Herbs and spices are vital when it comes to preparing foods but they tend to collect over time and end up expiring. First of all, take stock of your spice rack: use only spices that are most often employed in the kitchen and stay fresh. A fun way to declutter is by turning it into a game: consume half a glass of water and then go to the kitchen to find the oldest spice in the pantry and empty the container. It not only results in less mess around the house but also makes the food you eat as savory as possible. These are some important tips on maintaining the spice rack; it is recommendable to point out that checking the dates of explication is important. It is a simple habit that makes your pantry useful when you feel like experimenting with recipes. You may think that a simple task such as cleaning up your spice rack will not make a huge deal, but it will make a great difference when it comes to the functionality and even the taste of your meals, to have a kitchen to back up your culinary aptitude.

Gadget Overload

Kitchen gadgets are designed to help us prepare food and are helpful, but they are notorious for accumulating in every corner of the kitchen if not well managed. First, identify the usefulness of the gadget – if it has not been used for the previous year then, it is high time that it should be discarded. It can be suggested to give away any gadgets you do not need anymore to somebody who can use them. To have the functionality you want in a place, yet make the place compact, it makes sense to opt for multi-functional tools. For instance, a good quality chef's knife can do the work of many other knives, and a hard-wearing blender does similar work. When you narrow down your kitchen accessories you make your cooking operation easier and your kitchen less cluttered. The idea here is to end up with a kitchen that has basic cookery tools that you often have to use so that the experience of cooking becomes a lot more fun and the kitchen a more pleasant and orderly place to be.

Day 3-4:
Set Specific Goals for Your Decluttering Journey

Checklist Areas to Focus On	Check
Old receipts you won't use in tax returns	[ ]
Broken hangers	[ ]
Expired medicine or vitamins	[ ]
Empty shampoo bottles	[ ]
Expired canned goods	[ ]
Worn-out shoes	[ ]
Broken eyeglasses & sunglasses	[ ]
Dried-up nail polish	[ ]
Rusted hair accessories	[ ]
Old toothbrushes and razors	[ ]
Expired sunscreen	[ ]
Stretched-out hair ties or bands	[ ]
Old phone cases and chargers	[ ]
Random pieces of paper, notes, and sticky notes	[ ]
Junk mail and old catalogs	[ ]
Goals to Set	**Check**
Identify three areas in your home that will benefit most from decluttering.	[ ]
Set clear and achievable targets for each area.	[ ]
Write down your specific decluttering goals.	[ ]
Create a timeline for completing each area.	[ ]
Prioritize areas that cause the most stress or overwhelm.	[ ]
Break down large areas into smaller, manageable tasks.	[ ]

Living Rooms: The Battle of the Remote Controls and Dust Bunnies

Introduction to Living Room Decluttering

The living room is a special space that is central to the home as it is a place where people share time, laugh, and have fun. But it's easily possible for it to turn into a symbol of mess, where remotes tend to go 'missing' and dust gathers in corners. It is a snowball of small annoyances that begin to make a room look organized and cluttered. To keep the living room harmonious, it is critical to get rid of chaos and clutter. Start by asking yourself: The question that should be answered is: 'What mood do I want in my living room?' From this question, you will be able to better steer your goals when designing living rooms toward providing a place where people can engage with one another or chill. As you think of removing some items from your living room, bear in mind that a clean and tidy living room not only makes the physical room far more useful, but it also makes the entire house environment to be more relaxing and comfortable for one and all.

Remote Control Headquarters

Early models of remote controls are notorious for going missing at the exact moments that people feel that they most require them. To overcome this issue, separate an area for all the remotes—professionals call this space a 'remote graveyard'. It is possible to place the snacks in a decorative basket or a small tray that will be located at the coffee table. To enhance this even further, decorate the basket with a 'Welcome Home!' sign or words to that effect as well as 'Home of the Remotes' written on it in large font to make all members of the household return the remote control to the basket. If one has, for instance, smart lamps and television, they may opt for apps that combine the control panel, thus, few remotes will be required. Each heaped together also frees up from the daily chase in searching for the remotes as they are well arranged. Ask yourself: "If I were conscious of the location of the remotes instantly how much time could be saved?" This might just provide you with the incentive you need to plan and implement a central universal remote control system.

Combating Dust Bunnies

Dust bunnies prefer hidden areas that are mostly out of sight such as under furniture or furniture corners. With the presence of germs and bacteria, it is very important to set a time for cleaning to get rid of them and have a clean environment. Engage everybody in the cleaning process and make cleaning challenges – who will gather and remove the most dust balls? This becomes less of a chore when little incentives are given which may include children. One should also not forget to dust behind and under furniture, since dust bunnies' favorite places are behind any furniture. Just the other day, a basic question such as, 'When was it that you last dusted under the couch?' helps prod you to clean those obscure areas. Alone in dealing with dust bunnies makes the living room clean and enhances the quality of air hence making the atmosphere in the room more conducive for everybody.

Decluttering Furniture and Decorations

A messy living room looks and feels confined, but when a minimalist approach is incorporated, the living room becomes airy and calming. The first order of business is to look at each of the pieces of furniture – do you need them? Do they make you happy? Discard the things that do not serve a purpose, as well as those that are not beneficial when it comes to the aesthetic sense of the room. About ornamental items, the adage, 'the less the merrier' is probably the most appropriate. Learn the art of selection when it comes to decorating your space- do not put up an item that will not make you smile, feel good in your skin, or bring you good memories. A prompt to guide this process might be: It directly puts into your mind this question: Does this item add value to my interior space or is it a mere clutter? By doing this, you create space, and everyone loves a spacious home. This is even made better with the understanding that all the decorations have a place so that the living room is a comfortable and quiet place to be.

Day 5-7: Create a Vision Board or Journal Entry

Items to Reflect On	Check
Expired coupons	[ ]
Old & worn-out shoes	[ ]
Broken eyeglasses & sunglasses	[ ]
Dried-up nail polish	[ ]
Rusted hair accessories	[ ]
Empty disposable cups	[ ]
Old magazines and newspapers	[ ]
Outdated electronics and chargers	[ ]
Burnt-out candles	[ ]
Expired pantry items	[ ]
Broken or mismatched Tupperware lids	[ ]
Unused kitchen gadgets	[ ]

Vision Board Ideas	Check
Use images that represent a clutter-free, peaceful home.	[ ]
Include motivational quotes that resonate with your goals.	[ ]
Add photos of organized, minimalist spaces that inspire you.	[ ]
Incorporate symbols or words that reflect your decluttering goals.	[ ]
Create a digital vision board if you prefer an electronic format.	[ ]
Review and update your vision board regularly to stay motivated.	[ ]

Journal Prompts	Check
What items do you envision in your ideal space?	[ ]
How will a decluttered environment improve your daily life?	[ ]
What emotions do you want to feel in your space (e.g., peace, joy, clarity)?	[ ]
How do you plan to maintain your decluttered space long-term?	[ ]
What challenges do you anticipate, and how will you overcome them?	[ ]

Action	Check
1. Complete your vision board or journal entry, focusing on the transformation you desire.	[ ]
2. Review your goals and adjust your plan if necessary.	[ ]
Reflect on your progress and celebrate the steps you've taken so far.	[ ]

Emotional and Practical Benefits of Room-Specific Decluttering

Mental Clarity

Clutter is one of the best sources of stress and clearing it creates a good environment for the mind to focus. When people arrange their environment, thoughts do not work on germinating creative ideas and instead are free to undertake their daily duties. Just thinking about walking into a clean house after work — there is a feeling of relaxation; one can take a deep breath. This has a logic of restoring the concentration and focus of a human being hence facilitating the completion of tasks with efficiency being achieved.

Hint: Maintain a decluttering journal to document your productivity as well as the effects of the behavioral changes that you gain from the process. This is why documenting your progress is not only motivational but also keeps reminding you of the clear mind that comes with an organized environment. It also helps when you look at your journal from time to time to refresh your memory on why it is important to declutter your home to achieve orderliness so that you can be focused on the things that matter in life.

Emotional Well-Being

We can define decluttering as not only the removal of physical clutter but also of emotional clutter. Stress in an organization makes it easier to discharge the burden of previous experiences to be happier in the present. Clutter is the same as mental clutter, and when you remove everything that fills your space, you're removing what fills your head as well.

Guidance: Now think about how decluttering has affected you in terms of how you feel about yourself. Did you ever observe that there has been a certain elevation of spirits in the household? Do you have a sense that you are paying increased attention to the objects that you want to possess? Consider this as a transition to a purposeful and happy life. Minimalism is about not simply less quantity but less – less of the things that don't make us happy. If you are still in the process of decluttering, remember that it's the emotional liberation that you should embrace further on.

Physical Health

A clean home is not only one that lacks a lot of stuff; it is also one that is beneficial to your health. This saves on time and makes cleaning more efficient hence creating a disease-free living space. A neat environment implies that there are no pile-ups that can harbor dust and hence, make a big improvement in the quality of air to aspects concerning welfare.

Encouragement: Think of how healthy you are becoming because of the efforts that you are making to declutter your home. How much less time and effort does it take to clean the place, and how much has the air freshness changed for the better in your home? Consider how these changes benefit your body in general—it may be something simple like being able to breathe and that allergies are not a problem to you. Whenever you are washing or making the arrangement try to remind yourself and think how these are benefiting you by making the home healthier. You do not just get to improve your living conditions, but you also ensure that you are provided a sound body and mind in the long run due to the reduced level of clutter.

Improved Relationships

Discluttering penetrates our lives and can affect our relationships significantly. Clutter-free environment enhances proper living because the occupants of a home will not be likely to quarrel over lost items and dirty places which are always a common source of conflict. Because then, toys do not clutter the room or a play area, and, therefore, leave space, not only physically, but also mentally, for interactions with close ones.

Hint: Decluttering should be done alongside other family members; the individual should consider it as an opportunity to spend time with your loved ones. If possible, transform it into a group where everyone can join and help in organizing the home. Such division of work does help make the work less cumbersome and at the same time improves teamwork and cooperation. Working on this process with your significant other, you will notice that cleaning up unites you, as well as gives a sense of satisfaction. Of course, happiness at home is the key to sound personal relations in the family. Thus, fostering community draws people in where they are, and in doing so, you are caring for the relationships that are most important in life – peace and order.

Conclusion

Recap of Room-Specific Decluttering

When decluttering, it is essential to consider that it is not about cleaning each room without any plan. Hence the strategies include, defining the core purpose of the space, for instance, whether it is the bedroom, kitchen, living space, or bathroom, and storing only what is necessary, sorting and categorizing the rest. When you divide the process into individual rooms, you add a level of control and efficiency which will help you declutter. Do not forget that cleaning means achieving order that brings harmony and productivity into one's life and everyone's experience here should reflect this ultimate aim.

Embracing the Process

It's possible to make 'decluttering' a rewarding process if only people add some humor to it and don't frown at the process. Shouldn't we be able to have a good laugh at the situation and fight the 'monsters' step by step as Homer does? Learn indeed to live with it and be okay with the errors that come with the new change; rejoice in the small milestones that are achieved in the process. When we focus on decluttering as a long process and not just a one-day event, we start setting ourselves for victory and get to enjoy the process much more.

Looking Forward

A decluttered home offers numerous benefits: Free of stress, easy to manage, and more openness to the things and people you want around. When you are going to practice the minimalist way of life, bear in mind that every single change is a step toward the goal you have set for yourself. The continuous process of minimizing the complexity of the environment is not going to improve your physical surroundings alone but is also going to lead to a happier and healthier life.

Chapter 4: Decluttering for Families: Kid-Friendly Strategies to Tidy Up (Without Losing Your Mind)

The Great Toy Takeover: How to Regain Control

Introduction to Toy Chaos

I do not know how toys reproduce themselves and appear in various rooms of the house, turning the living areas into fairytale-like messes. Toys are crucial in every play and learning activity but like most things, if not well monitored, they become an issue for parents and children alike. Leaning on a misplaced LEGO is a human way of being told one has to get back in control again. However, beyond the points of discomfort it causes, other issues stem from having excess toys including that it leads to the kid having a cluttered mind as they struggle to have a great time playing. If you are ready to begin the process of retaking your home it is very important to create a toy box or, as some parents call it, a Toy Zone. **Hint:** The very first step to attaining a living room that does not resemble a war zone after the children have played with their toys is to create a Toy Zone.

Creating a Toy Zone

To reduce the confusion that comes with having toys all over the place, it is advisable to make a dedicated play zone. Simply having a corner, a shelf, or some bins to contain toys aids in setting the tone of the room for playtime, and where toys are kept, is where playtime occurs. Divisions are, of course, important – use a rug, a piece of furniture, or if you wish, some fun-colored adhesive tape on the floor to divide it. Not only do the toys not spread around but cleaning them up is extremely easy as well too as they are separated. **Guidance:** Let your children help decide and arrange their Toy Zone. If allowed to partake in the process, they are more capable of owning it and ensuring it is clean. **Encouragement:** Making the concept of a Toy Zone is not solely to avoid the number it is just important to provide your children with a space where they can play to their extent as well as let them learn the importance of tidiness.

The "One In, One Out" Rule

To keep the toy clutter under control, implement the "One In, One Out" rule: it was their rule that the number of toys could not increase in the house – for every new toy that comes to live in the house, one must depart. One way of achieving this is by deploying the 'one in, one out' rule, which keeps the number of toys under control while, at the same time, nurturing the child's decision-making skills. Let your children decide which toys should remain in their playroom and which should be donated, ideally, set them the task. **Prompt:** One can ask for example, "Which toy have you outgrown/ no longer play with?" This makes the child consider what he or she has and make reasonable decisions. **Benefits:** Thus, by following this rule, you do not overload toys and at the same time teach your kids responsibility. They realize that space is limited and that giving away the toys they no longer play with creates space for newer toys they would love to possess, again, overconsumption is discouraged.

Creative Storage Solutions

Children like to tidy up their messes but the fun of tidying up decays when they are so bored due to repetition, hence, brings out creativity and makes tidying up interesting with ideas on how to store those items that are to be tidied. Using DIY toy chests, colored baskets, and personalized storage boxes can turn the task of having to clean the toys into a fun activity. Let your children be the ones to choose how the storage options should look– this brings creativity into play and makes the children more willing to use the storage more frequently than they usually would. **Hint:** To give a new look and interest to your toy, paint an old bookshelf along with your kids. Guidance: Explain to your child that storage is not boring but it is fun and part of the play. Indeed when they feel that their storage solutions are part of them they are more encouraged to maintain their toys. **Encouragement:** Apart from that, creative storage does the job of not only storing toys but also making tidiness fun and being a part of your home's aesthetics.

Dealing with Emotional Attachments

Children ascribe meaning and importance to toys, thus it becomes painful for them to give out toys. These are important attachments that should be honored while at the same time encouraging the discarding of clutter. As much as this may be painful, one can reduce the process by taking pictures of toys that have sentimental value. This makes it possible for your child to retain the feeling related to the object but not possess the material thing. Another idea is to make a Memory Box – the toys that are especially dear to the kid are placed there and are well-guarded. **Prompt:** I recommend the following question to your child: "Which toys are the most dear to you?" This would make your child stop overthinking and help them make decisions as to what should be stored. **Guidance:** Assure your child that it is acceptable to give some toys to others to play with because the memories of those toys are with the child in mind and the pictures. **Encouragement:** Therefore, by as much as you assist the child in rationalizing, you make it easier for him to let go of his clutter since he moves with the understanding that although the physical objects are let go, the memories remain.

Day 8-10:
Reflect on Emotional Attachments

Items to Reflect On	Check
Blurry photos that you never look at	[ ]
Old letters or greeting cards	[ ]
Childhood toys or keepsakes	[ ]
Gifts from people you're no longer in touch with	[ ]
Souvenirs from trips or events you barely remember	[ ]
Outgrown clothing that holds memories	[ ]
Family heirlooms that don't fit your current lifestyle	[ ]
Books you keep for sentimental reasons but never read	[ ]
Old art projects or schoolwork	[ ]
Duplicate items with emotional ties	[ ]
Old diaries or journals that no longer reflect who you are	[ ]
Photos of people or places that evoke negative feelings	[ ]

Questions to Consider	Check
Does this item bring me joy or hold me back?	[ ]
Am I holding onto this because I feel guilty about letting it go?	[ ]
Would I choose to keep this if I were starting fresh?	[ ]
Is this item enhancing my life or adding to my clutter?	[ ]
Can I honor the memory without holding onto the physical item?	[ ]

Action	Check
Take photos of sentimental items before letting them go.	[ ]
Write about the memories attached to items in a journal.	[ ]
Consider donating or gifting sentimental items to someone who will appreciate them.	[ ]
Reflect on how letting go of these items can make space for new experiences.	[ ]
Create a memory box for the most cherished items.	[ ]

Involving Kids in the Process: Turning Decluttering into a Game (With Prizes!)

Making Decluttering Fun

Challenge yourself and your family, to make decluttering an enjoyable process by making it into a game. Explain the situation with your kids as a scavenger hunt where they can find 'hidden' treasures – toys that have been neglected for some time. The trick here is to set up challenges and rewards neatly: make a vibrant chart of jobs such as 'get five toys to donate' or 'place the books in the corresponding color.' When the child does the task right, they get a small prize. **Hint:** You can use stickers, points, or even extra playtime as a reward. **Guidance:** Motivate your kids to clean up by telling them that they are on a mission and that is to make their room more fun. **Encouragement:** To encourage kids to declutter and follow the example, it is necessary to make the process as entertaining and as appealing as a game, so the children understand that tidiness is as enjoyable as the game before naptime. This means making them develop a positive attitude towards cleaning which would be anathema to them as they would approach the chore with a lot of reluctance.

Family Competition

It may sound silly, but turn the process of decluttering the rooms into a competition by dividing the rooms among the family members, so that it becomes more like a game. They should then be given a time limit then they will have to compete on the amount of time it takes them to organize the space. Two goals consist of the first to the finish line or the one who cleans the most objects in the office wins. **Prompt:** For example, when calling on students to look for toys to donate say, "Who can find the most toys in the next 10 minutes?" **Guidance:** Stress that it is not a race and one has to wash every area as one wants to leave it as clean as possible. **Encouragement:** Cohort competition breathes life into this activity making decluttering much more fascinating in the context of family competitions. It also makes provision for teamwork and cooperation since everyone is striving towards achieving the same objective. Moreover, it is a good opportunity to become closer while arranging the dwelling place of the family.

Teaching Generosity and Sustainability

It is also important to teach your children the values of generosity as well as the need for sustainability whenever you are decluttering. Organize a children's fun toy and item collection whereby children decide on toys and items they no longer play with and give them to those in needy considerate households. To make it more fun, allow them to draw, stick, and glitter any box that you want to be a donation box to make it a form of artwork. **Hint:** Illustrate to them how their old toys can also make other children happy, and make them appreciate the aspect of sharing. **Guidance:** Remind them, "Just think, how much joy another child will get playing with this toy." **Encouragement:** teaching the children about the environmental impact of what they are doing and the importance of giving back to the community is also a key concept that is part of this process. This reassures the children that whenever they share their toys and other products they are helping the world to become a better place.

Celebrating the Victory

All the hard work has to be rewarded: It is time to have fun! Hold a very short 'celebration' to formally acknowledge all the participants' efforts by distributing 'medals' – simple certificates or trophies or a small treat. You can also parade a success where children can proudly present to you the tightened spaces that they have, this will draw focus on the children. **Prompt:** Question your kids and ask them how it feels to see their rooms so clean and organized, this is to ensure that the children understand that they have benefitted from the cleaning exercises. **Guidance:** Let them know that organizing is not a mere washing exercise—it's organizing their space to make it comfortable for them. **Encouragement:** It does help to acknowledge achievements regardless of how trivial they may be as this goes a long way in encouraging the right things to be done and the act of decluttering of being enjoyable. They get to learn that their work is being appreciated and that they have to feel proud of what they have done and that is to have a nice and clean space to play in.

Maintaining a Clutter-Free Home with Kids

Establishing Daily Routines

Children should be encouraged to adopt certain discipline when tidying up their spaces to ensure a clean home. Scheduling time in the day to clean, before dinner, or right before bed helps teach children responsibility. Maintenance is very important—make cleaning time fun; for instance, let children on the clean-up race or the child who tidies up the most toys before the clock reaches a certain point. **Hint:** Make clean-up fun by playing the most preferred song of the child during this time. **Guidance:** Tell them that a clean environment or house is comfortable to play or even relax in thus improving their experiences. **Encouragement:** The establishment of these routines contributes towards the setting up of an organized home without feeling like is a tedious task all the time. Another aspect of the show is teaching children that little daily changes can translate into a big positive change at the end of the week; decluttering becomes easy and a part of children's daily routine.

Seasonal Decluttering

Teach your family to adopt seasonal decluttering as a habit by ensuring that there is a designated clean-out session at the beginning of every season. With these check-ups happening every three months, parents are presented with a perfect chance to go through the many toys and belongings of their children, and sort between those they need to keep, those they can donate, and those that should be recycled. This is a perfect time given that your needs change with the specific seasons in a particular year regarding organization and cluttering of your home. **Prompt:** Question your child by saying, "Which toys are you still using, and which are no longer useful for you?" This will make the child to reason among themselves. **Guidance:** Illustrate the point that it is easier to let go of certain items that are not suitable for a particular season to allow for others that are more suitable for the upcoming season. **Encouragement:** Seasonal cleaning is useful to avoid the home becoming overrun by unnecessary things that have not been used for a long time and to prepare it for the optimistic associations that each new season brings.

Encouraging Mindfulness

Children need to learn to avoid overconsumption to avoid the accumulation of clutter in the house. Teach them the meaning of the phrase 'one man's trash is another man's treasure, by making them consider carefully before they bring new toys or other possessions into the house. Hence the need to remind them that time and again they should consider shifts from owning material things to considering the experiences they have had. **Prompt:** Question, "Do you really need this, or would you rather save for something special or spend time doing something fun?" **Counseling:** share your own experience of the fact that the choice of an experience is much more rewarding than the purchase of a thing. **Encouragement:** The concept of mindfulness ensures the kids learn about the things they possess and ensures there is less desire to acquire more things that lead to more clutter. In the long run, it creates satisfaction and thankfulness, and your home becomes a place very deliberately thought through.

Parental Involvement

For parents, modeling or showing how they could declutter and arrange their items can be one of the most helpful strategies. So, if you make it a point to daily or weekly tidy up your surrounding spaces daily and make intelligent choices of what to keep and what not to, children shall be able to emulate you. Make decluttering a family affair – when a house is decluttered by many people it becomes easier and the something that brings the family together in activity. **Hint:** Organise a family decluttering day for the family in which tasks are assigned to the different rooms of the house. **Guidance:** Let your children learn that tidiness is not just about washing – tidying means that everybody is going to be fine in this home. **Encouragement:** Parental involvement makes it easier for decluttering to be seen by everybody as a collective exercise that has the backing of everybody in the compound. By encouraging everyone to participate in keeping the environment clean, there is a feeling of ownership hence people will not tolerate cluttering.

Day 11-12:
Research Decision Fatigue

Questions to Explore	Check
How does decision fatigue impact my daily life?	[ ]
Do I feel overwhelmed by the number of choices I have to make?	[ ]
How does clutter contribute to my decision fatigue?	[ ]
What are the signs of decision fatigue I experience regularly?	[ ]
How does decision fatigue affect my ability to declutter?	[ ]
Research Ideas	**Check**
Read about the psychology behind decision fatigue.	[ ]
Explore strategies for reducing decision fatigue in everyday life.	[ ]
Watch videos on simplifying decision-making processes.	[ ]
Look into how clutter can exacerbate decision fatigue.	[ ]
Study minimalist approaches to reducing mental load.	[ ]
Action	**Check**
Implement strategies to reduce decision fatigue (e.g., routines, minimizing choices).	[ ]
Declutter areas that contribute most to decision fatigue (e.g., closets, kitchen).	[ ]
Practice making quick, decisive choices in small areas first.	[ ]
Simplify your environment to reduce the number of decisions you need to make.	[ ]
Reflect on how these changes make you feel more in control and less overwhelmed.	[ ]

The Long-Term Benefits of Decluttering for Families

Enhanced Family Relationships

Clutter-free home plays a crucial role in improving family relations because most conflicts that arise from stress arise from missing stuff and messy environments. You find yourself chasing things and elements much less often and spend more precious time actually playing with your child, eating dinner together, or even just being in a clean and pristine home. **Hint:** Think of having free time to shop for the family and engage in other family undertakings instead of organizing the house – that is made possible by decluttering. **Guidance:** Get your family to appreciate that chaos only serves to reduce the quality of time spent on things that matter. **Encouragement:** It does mean a home free of clutter creates more improved togetherness among family members and results in improving the well-being of the family members.

Improved Mental Health

Decluttering enhances the quality of living standards by bringing out a good feeling about the environment to be cleaned and specific to a room, cleaning reduces anxiety. The clutter-free environment helps everyone to be more attentive to work, interests, hobbies, and time spent together, displacing the clutter. **Prompt:** One should ask oneself a question: 'How does it feel to live in a clean room, in an environment free from clutters?"; an answer to this question could be the primary motivating factor behind regular cleaning. **Guidance:** Tell your family that the decision to declutter leads to a clear mind. **Encouragement:** When the house is clean, you set yourself for a constructive mental healthy framework that is productive for parents and friends as well as the young ones. The order in a home or room transfers to every other aspect of life hence has an easier time handling other stresses in life.

Healthier Living Environment

Clutter not only looks bad but also is bad for you: That's why a clean home can make all the difference. When there are fewer objects it is much simpler to maintain cleanness and exclude such irritants as dust and mite allergens. Daily space clearance facilitates the cleaning process and hence your domicile is a safe and healthy place for your kinfolk. **Hint:** Consider how simple chores such as vacuuming and dusting are when you don't have various items on your furniture and floors. **Guidance:** It is also important to explain to your children that by getting rid of clutter you get a cleaner, healthier environment for your children to play and develop in. **Encouragement:** The organization of the house entails cleaning, and removing items that are not essential to create comfort and enhance the health of the family members. By focusing on such an approach to maintaining the home, the worth of the home is not only seen in the aspect of physical health, but the occupants also take pride in owning the space.

Teaching Valuable Life Skills

There are several benefits that children can get from decluttering which include; Responsibility, Organization, and Environmental stewardship. Children learn a lot from the process, for example, the little ones get to learn how to protect their possessions and make decisions on things they want to keep or discard, and other things, they learn about the benefits of donating or recycling. **Prompt:** You might ask your child such a question as, "What can you do to make your room clean and a place you would be proud of?" The question will get them to contemplate clutter and its real effects and the advantages of tidiness. **Guidance:** Further explain to them that in such practice they are going to be preparing for lifetime or regular habits that they are going to practice when they become adults. **Encouragement:** From this, it can be deduced that children who learn how to manage their territory help themselves by being responsible taking responsibility, and being independent all through their adulthood. They are raised learning fundamental tenets such as frugality and environmental conservation, which are critical pillars for a content life.

Conclusion

Recap of Strategies: Some of the ideas used when decluttering with kids include; Daily pick-ups, using play mats, the 'one in one out' rule, and child involvement in organizing and storage are some effective ways to deal with toy clutter. By organizing a clean-up operation each spring cleaning, mindfulness exercises as well as involving parents drive the perception of a cluttered environment and thus prevent the accumulation of clutter during the year.

Embracing the Journey: As already pointed it cleaning is not a boring process so when decluttering one is also making it a fulfilling process, especially when done together with the family. Handling clean-up as playtime and getting all members of any familial unit involved makes cleaning up an activity that fosters unity of the family unit. Accept it with a light heart and look at every effort as leading to a neater and calmer home environment.

Looking Forward: Housing cleanliness is not a one-time reward since a clean house means that there will not be clutter to sort through. It promotes a happier healthier upbringing for children, by lessening stress, improving the mental wellness of the family, and providing cleanliness. Cultivating these habits will extend into the future as useful principles for a healthy life, free from the unnecessary complications that a large family may introduce in a household.

Chapter 5:
Digital Decluttering: Because Your Phone Doesn't Need 8,000 Photos of Your Cat

Organizing Your Devices: The Quest for the Holy Grail of Storage

The Desktop of Doom

Digital clutter is as bad as physical clutter and this is evident most often by the condition of one's computer desktop. Well-organized files, screenshots, and often-used shortcuts can pile up over a period and in the end, the desktop becomes more or less similar to a cluttered drawer in the kitchen. Clutters not only reduce your efficiency but also create extra pressure you do not need. **Hint:** Just think of what it would be like to open your computer and have a clean and properly organized desktop—the simple sight of it gives motivation. **Guidance:** First and foremost, it is necessary to become minimalistic – do not use the desktop as a place to store files, but rather as the starting platform for work. Time and again, sort through the items so that you take what you need and use most often. **Encouragement:** When you clean your desktop you erect a blank canvas and this gives you a fresh outlook in organizing your experiences and making your computer usage a lot more enjoyable.

Streamlining Applications

People install applications as they come across them and many of them are rarely used, while others occupy space on the device's memory. The first step is to determine what has some utility and what does not, as there is usually a long list of installed applications. **Prompt:** Just recently, I followed this rule:

read through the list of apps on your phone and ask yourself "When was the last time I used this app?" **Hint:** It's like having the clean-up before spring cleaning of your phone or computer. **Guidance:** Instead of having a list of hundreds of apps where some of which are rarely used but occupy a lot of space, try to have a few of the most commonly used applications as well as those that provide the users with mindful utilities and benefits. **Encouragement:** Cleaning up those apps also saves space while also ensuring you are only left with the apps that are relevant and useful to you, distressing your digital life and decision fatigue.

Managing Digital Files

Similarly to the physical items, files may accumulate in the digital environment and it may become a struggle to locate something or access it as required. It is thus important to from time to time go through documents that are no longer relevant and which one would not need to use ever again in a process we shall term the digital funeral. **Prompt:** Perhaps, it will be useful to follow the schedule and free space on the computer once a week removing unnecessary files. **Hint:** Make this into a habit, or a ritual to do, maybe with a cup of coffee to drink while listening to soothing music. **Guidance:** In case of the files containing some special memories, then you can keep a scrapbook digital as a way of dealing with clutter. **Encouragement:** Not only can you ensure that you will regain space in your computer, laptop, or external hard drive, but you can also reduce stress due to a confused mess of files on your computer.

Using Cloud Storage Effectively

Cloud storage is a marvelous resource for neatening up one's electronic life but it can easily turn into a gigantic wasteland of digital clutter unless properly regulated. First, easier to recognize the advantages and possible disadvantages of cloud storage – advertised as a way to save space on devices, but it actually can be really helpful only if used properly. **Hint:** Do not consider that putting files in cloud storage eliminates the need to uninstall applications or delete unnecessary data. **Guidance:** Categorize your files in the cloud storage and also check what you saved from time to time. **Prompt:** Questions to ask yourself; Is that file really necessary to be on my computer or just clutter? Cloud utilization: As the reality of digital life continues to unfold, keeping the digital life under control and easily searchable relieves one of the stressors associated with it.

Day 13-14:
Identify Habits That Contribute to Clutter

Habits to Identify	Check
Leaving items out instead of putting them away	[ ]
Shopping as a way to relieve stress	[ ]
Accumulating items because they were on sale	[ ]
Keeping duplicates "just in case"	[ ]
Postponing decisions on items (e.g., mail, magazines)	[ ]
Allowing paper clutter to pile up without sorting it	[ ]
Buying new items without discarding old ones	[ ]
Failing to regularly review and declutter possessions	[ ]
Holding onto broken items to fix them someday	[ ]
Saving items out of fear of future need (e.g., old cables, packaging)	[ ]
Keeping items that no longer serve a purpose but are "too good" to throw away	[ ]

Questions to Consider	Check
Which habits contribute most to the clutter in my life?	[ ]
How can I replace these habits with more productive ones?	[ ]
What routines can I establish to maintain a clutter-free environment?	[ ]
How can I be more mindful about what I bring into my home?	[ ]
What triggers my clutter-inducing habits, and how can I address them?	[ ]

Action	Check
Identify one habit to change each week and track your progress.	[ ]
Replace a clutter-inducing habit with a minimalist habit (e.g., "one in, one out" rule).	[ ]
Set up regular decluttering sessions to prevent accumulation.	[ ]
Create a designated space for items that need to be sorted or dealt with.	[ ]
Reflect on how these new habits align with your minimalist goals.	[ ]

Digital Files: How to Avoid the Black Hole of Unwanted Documents

Effective Naming Conventions

Among all actions of digital clutter removal, the process of file naming is among the most basic yet highly effective. The criteria of file naming is one of the simplest and most effective means for reducing stress while looking for a particular file. **Prompt:** Before saving a file, one should ask whether he will know what this is in the next six months. They should use descriptive names for the files and add the dates when they reach for them later. Doing this should become habitual; that is, all files should be named uniformly according to their format. **Encouragement:** Correctly named files do contribute to the organization of your digital life but also eliminate the time-consuming activity of wading through unlabeled files.

Creating an Organized File System

In order not to succumb to the black hole of papers unwanted, there is a need for an organization system. Begin with the creation of a folder structure that would suit your needs, whether it will be work, personal, or hobby files, or files by year and the projects performed. **Hint:** The arrangements of your folders should be thought of as virtual systems of filing cabinets each of which have a specific function. **Guidance:** Subdividing into greater categories is also possible; in any case, care should be taken to practice regular cleaning. **Prompt:** Put a note to yourself to go through your files and organize them at least once a month. **Encouragement:** Not only do clean files save the would-be wasted time but it also reduces the anxiety that comes from knowing that one has a complete mess in their digital organization.

Regular Digital Maintenance

As with the physical offices, the clutter recurs only if one does not maintain the digital space regularly. A specific slot within a given month should be devoted to checking and organizing the pile of documents on the computer. **Hint:** This may be as basic as winding up every month with 15 minutes dedicated to some work downtime. **Guidance:** When carrying out such a step, it is advisable to remove files that you do not require in the current or near future and organize well the remaining documents. **Prompt:** You should also ask, is this file still necessary to be on my computer? If you find none then, you should delete the file. **Encouragement:** Digital House Cleaning simply maintains your online presence, helps to lessen the strain, and makes the tools simpler so you can center on the important things.

Utilizing Digital Decluttering Tools

Today, quite many applications and programs can make the organizing and managing of files easier. These latter tools may help at least some of the processes of clearing out and finding similar files. **Hint:** If you are to use a particular type of file, then it will be more appropriate to invest in a tool that best suits that type. **Guidance:** Even if these tools are very useful, do not overuse them all the time. Even here, the files should still be provincially checked to prevent any important files from being deleted. Encouragement: Therefore, when using these organization technologies, the process can be made simpler and quicker to keep your digital spaces tidy.

The Benefits of Digital Decluttering

Enhanced Productivity

Clutter is always an enemy of efficiency and exactly web space is one such problem that we could encounter. When your desktop has become crowded with icons and folders, and when your folders have become packed with unsorted documents, concentration is difficult. When you have removed the physical apps, what is left is a neater interface that is ideal for use in the enhancement of focus and organization. **Hint:** First and foremost, it is recommended to separate the most often-used files into neat folders that will be convenient to open. This basic action can have a profound impact on how fast the particular file you are most interested in can be located. **Guidance:** It is important to sustain this faculty and this is best achieved by persistently deleting files on download, and documents saved on the desktop. **Encouragement:** It is helpful to view digital decluttering as an approach to optimize what we do in our daily lives so that we can do these more effectively with more focused minds. If one's online environment is clean and orderly, then one's head is also clean and orderly, and, correspondingly, work will be more efficient and enjoyable.

Emotional Well-Being

I think that just as chairs piling up can put physical pressure on your mind, so can files and emails and a million small tasks. It is quite frustrating to look for the files that were downloaded or the apps that were installed but are no longer used frequently. Thus, by cleaning up your digital environment you minimize this burden which in return gives a sense of orderliness. **Prompt:** Have you ever felt good when your current folder inbox is empty or your desktop is devoid of files? Yes, it is a kind of achievement! **Guidance:** Spare one day a week to organize and discard specific emails, applications, or documents depending on the clutter's extent. **Encouragement:** Do not forget, that decluttering in the digital world is as liberating as decluttering the physical space. They don't just mean clearing the clutter on your desks and counters; it means clearing your head for a space for order in your life.

Physical Device Performance

More than hindering your productivity, digital clutter hinders the speed of your computer or any other device. With time different files that are not often used, extra applications, and even data can cause the device to slow down and use more resources than it is supposed to. Cleaning and tidiness of devices play a vital role in the device's speed, durability as well as free space in it. **Hint:** It's a good idea to designate a week's reminder to clean up your device—remove unnecessary applications that have accumulated over the months, and free up cache files. **Guidance:** Think about your handheld device as any other instrument; it will give the best results if well managed. **Encouragement:** An uncluttered device can perform better and you are less likely to experience crashes or storage-related problems. In this way, you have cleaned your space of them and thus you are making sure that you make your devices work efficiently for many years.

Better Digital Hygiene

Having a clean space means no bad thing and can help in making sure your personal information remains safe. System and files should also be reviewed and old files deleted to prevent the exposure or loss of information. The organization also helps to reduce the risks of data loss because a person will always have ideas on the location of specific files. **Prompt:** Asking yourself questions such as, 'When did I last check my security settings or how long has it been since I backed up the files?' may come in handy here **Guidance:** Take regular digital health checkups to ascertain whether the software being used is updated or if the files have been securely saved. **Encouragement:** You can consider digital decluttering as one of the measures of digital health. stages analogous to cleaning your house because when you become ill, digital tidiness is essential for the safeguarding of privacy and personal information. This is not only effective in protecting your information but also makes you free from any worry.

Day 15-17:
Practice Mindfulness

Mindfulness Prompts	Check
Is this item adding value to my life right now?	[ ]
Does this item contribute to my overall well-being?	[ ]
How does keeping this item align with my current goals and values?	[ ]
Does this item support the life I want to lead?	[ ]
Am I holding onto this item out of fear or habit?	[ ]
How do I feel when I look at or use this item?	[ ]
Is this item part of my past, present, or future?	[ ]
Would I feel lighter and more at peace without this item?	[ ]
Can I visualize my space without this item?	[ ]
How does this item impact my daily routines?	[ ]

Mindful Decluttering Activities	Check
Take deep breaths before making decisions about each item.	[ ]
Spend a few moments reflecting on how each item makes you feel.	[ ]
Practice gratitude for items that have served their purpose.	[ ]
Meditate on your goals for a clutter-free space before beginning.	[ ]
Use visualization techniques to imagine your space without clutter.	[ ]
Incorporate mindful pauses during decluttering to reassess your feelings.	[ ]

Action	Check
Apply mindfulness techniques to your decluttering process.	[ ]
Let go of items that no longer serve you with a sense of peace.	[ ]
Keep only those items that bring value, joy, and purpose to your life.	[ ]
Journal about your experience practicing mindfulness during decluttering.	[ ]

Long-Term Strategies for Maintaining a Decluttered Digital Life

Developing Consistent Habits

For a clutterless working environment especially when organizing documents using the digital approach one has to be consistent. Semantically, one should aim at formulating a disciplined system of cleaning up clutter; for instance, it is possible to dedicate some time every week to reorganizing files. **Hint:** Schedule breaks focused on the digital—now might be easiest to do every Sunday afternoon or the first Monday of the month. **Guidance:** Try to make digital decluttering as a routine as cleaning, to ensure that everything stays in order. To prevent clutter build-up, this is the routine to follow. **Encouragement:** Yes, this is the truth that hard works always pay. The above examples of perseverance illustrate this. It makes your work much less complicated in the long run when you're preserving your digital space, which minimizes the time spent on cleaning it later and helps to maintain its order and focus.

Seasonal Digital Decluttering

As with the cleaning that we do in our homes in spring, it is imperative to undertake the same in our digital houses. The following reviews help you modify organizational strategies to suit your present requirements and update your web space. **Prompt:** It is a good time to think, "What files or apps have I outgrown or no longer need this season?" **Guidance:** People should utilize the change of season as a reminder to declutter their digital life. This is important in avoiding the accumulation of additional files and applications which are unnecessary most of the time. **Encouragement:** In essence, you can consider the going through of your digital devices, an exercise in syncing with the emergent life. This is because with time the digital space becomes wielded and removes efficiency, thus by constantly editing the design you retain its effectiveness.

Mindful Digital Consumption

Living in the age of the Internet and endless opportunities to download or create new files, apps, and material, it is possible to accumulate all kinds of unnecessary items. This implies that the content that is downloaded or saved is done with the purpose of mindful consumption. **Hint:** For example, when you want to download a new application or a file, ask yourself whether you need it. The principles are simple, avoid quantity in favor of quality – pick content that will enrich your digital life. **Encouragement:** Placing penalties on the storage means that besides reducing clutter, you also improve the quality of the items and information stored. It assists in keeping one's environment free from clutter; both tangible and virtual, productive, and organized for a given purpose.

Embracing a Minimalist Digital Mindset

There are many advantages to taking the minimalist approach to your digital life. From the onset, accept the notion of having the fewest virtual items as possible—only those, which are meaningful and valuable. **Prompt:** Think about how much more calm and more managed your digital environment is when it is not full. **Guidance:** Simplify your physical and digital surroundings and exclude anything that is not essential in your life. **Encouragement:** Living intentionally in the digital space thus translates to less distraction, enhanced clarity, and focus. When you simplify, you establish an online setting that is conducive to executing your objectives and leading a better experience.

Conclusion

Recap of Digital Decluttering Benefits: Clearing your digital spaces provides a lot of advantages including increased work rates and device performances and better moods. It simply means that your office becomes less cluttered, productive stress is reduced and there is the benefit of knowing that your devices are optimally working as they should.

Embracing the Journey: It is important to understand that digital decluttering is not a linear task, but a process. Take it with laughter and vigor and remember that with each action for a cleaner virtual environment, life becomes more productive, less cluttered, and therefore more serene.

Looking Forward: When you keep on sustaining your neat and arranged virtual environment, you can expect more positive changes to occur. The need for structure organization and elimination of obstacles in the fast world will give you the quality of life that you need to have more time to do what is important to you.

Chapter 6: Seasonal Decluttering: Tackling Clutter with the Changing Seasons (Goodbye, Winter Coats!)

Spring Cleaning: The Annual Ritual of Dusting Off the Cobwebs

Introduction to Spring Cleaning

Whenever the days are longer and the cold of winter recedes, answering with the warmth of the returning sun, people are exposed to spring cleaning as a symbolic cleansing. It is not merely the cleanliness—it is the unburdening of ourselves to better start anew. Remember the Japanese TV show, where a woman named Marie Kondo is determined to declutter homes and bring the viewer's house a newfound, positive energy. Encapsulate your clutter into a reality show that desperately needs some makeover and give your space the much-needed decluttering and reorganization. **Hint:** It is a good point to start some type of a 'renewal' or a cleansing of the home and body. **Guidance:** Do not aim to start from scratch making it seem like you want to redo everything, it is best done slowly, and gradually, one room at a time. **Encouragement:** Such an approach of accepting this rite of passage makes it not only a clean-up endeavor, but allows for more color, order, and life.

Prioritizing Rooms

About spring cleaning, it is crucial to establish what I term the clutter zones, which are those parts of the house that are most rife with ordinarily used items. Lounges, kitchens, and bedrooms are the most used areas of a home and hence would be best to declutter. Begin with the bedroom, take your closet, for example, it is all go black hole that swallows everything whole, and who knows where everything is lodged. Next, heads to the kitchen, where one can work some magic and create an ordered environment by dealing with the spice cabinet and the pantry. Some good organizations include discarding stale products and organizing kitchen shelves in such a way that will not make cooking a burden. **Prompt:** Think, What room makes the most dramatic change if decluttered first **Guidance:** Try to work through one room at a time. **Encouragement:** Every room you clean gets you nearer and nearer to the home you desire which is that one that feels peaceful.

Family Involvement

Spring cleaning does not mean that one can perform it individually – gather everyone and turn it into a family activity. By getting everyone involved in the cleaning-up process, the load is well shared promoting teamwork as well. Engage the children in the process by making the decluttering a game or a competition; who can fill up a donors' box quicker? Or, who can point at the highest number of things that do not bring joy anymore? In this way, I succeeded at teaching a child the importance of tidiness and order as well as simplification of the work process while making the process interesting for a child. **Hint:** Continue to maintain a high level of motivation that brings into life a reward system for finished tasks. **Guidance:** This is also the best opportunity to instill responsibility and teach the child how to make a proper choice. **Encouragement:** Not only are you cleaning, but you are also making memories and teaching the values of purposing your life and creating purpose in one's life.

Digital Decluttering

It is not only the spaces in your house that require cleaning, even your digital life requires it during springtime. Managing digital mess is essential in the current world where documents, applications, and messages build up and can cause a lot of confusion. It is wise to begin the decluttering process by categorizing documents properly by creating good file folder names. Secondly, sort out your emails by deleting subscriptions with companies that are no longer relevant or necessary to your life. **Prompt:** Raise the same query, "When was the most recent that I opened this file or app?" **Guidance:** Just like your home, you should also schedule times for your spring cleaning in the digital world. **Encouragement:** Clutter in the digital space is not conducive to the enhancement of productivity; on the contrary, a clean and tidy virtual space offers a sense of mental well-being and helps to concentrate on the important things.

Day 18-19:

Gather Supplies

Essential Decluttering Supplies	Check
Sturdy boxes for sorting items	[ ]
Labels for categorizing boxes (e.g., "Donate," "Recycle," "Trash")	[ ]
Permanent markers for labeling	[ ]
Trash bags for discarding unwanted items	[ ]
Recycling bins for items that can be repurposed	[ ]
Cleaning supplies for dusting and wiping down surfaces	[ ]
Gloves to protect your hands during the process	[ ]
Measuring tape for evaluating storage spaces	[ ]
Bins or baskets for items to be relocated within the home	[ ]
Paper and pen for taking notes or making lists while decluttering	[ ]
Digital camera or phone to document progress or take "before and after" photos	[ ]

Areas to Focus On	Check
Kitchen drawers—remove old utensils, expired pantry items	[ ]
Bathroom cabinets—discard expired medications and toiletries	[ ]
Closet—sort through clothes, shoes, and accessories	[ ]
Home office—organize papers, old receipts, and outdated electronics	[ ]
Garage or storage—clear out tools, broken equipment, and unused items	[ ]
Laundry room—discard empty detergent bottles, mismatched socks	[ ]
Living room—organize books, DVDs, and unused decor	[ ]
Bedroom—remove old phone cases, chargers, and unused electronics	[ ]
Entryway or hallway—organize shoes, coats, and bags	[ ]
Kids' playroom—sort toys and games, discard broken or unused items	[ ]

Action	Check
Gather all necessary supplies before starting the decluttering process.	[ ]
Identify specific areas to focus on during your decluttering sessions.	[ ]
Make sure your decluttering space is well-organized and ready for the task ahead.	[ ]
Ensure you have everything needed to sort, organize, and dispose of items efficiently.	[ ]

Summer Decluttering: What to Do with All Those Flip-Flops

Introduction to Summer Decluttering

At some point during the winter season, one begins to notice that it is possible to own way too many flip-flops. This 'flip-flop crisis' can be liberating because it makes you come face to face with the reality of what you own. Round up all your flip-flops to one room and celebrate a 'flip-flop party' and you'll be surprised how many pairs of flip-flops you have collected in your lifetime. Well, ladies and gentlemen, it's time for a reality check – do you require all of the above? **Hint:** However, think about those pairs that you use and those pairs that you just leave in your wardrobe, or your closet all day. **Guidance:** To this task, openness should be applied, leaving behind all the useless footwear. **Encouragement:** Therefore, removing assorted flip-flops from your living space and sorting them is an acceptable way to become conscious of one's summer dressing conduct.

Sorting and Organizing

For those who still find it hard to let go, use the cutting-edge Marie Kondo method whereby one should keep only the flip-flops that are joyful and improve one's life. Appreciate the things that you have used, but don't be too attached to them; push away the things that you no longer use or do not fit your preference. You should think about sustainable spaces for the pairs that you wish to let go of. Slightly worn flip-flops can be donated, but other flip-flops may be upcycled in other ways. **Prompt:** The rule of thumb here would be, "Does this pair make me happy or do I have use for it?" Here, the great rule is to discard the things that you no longer use or wear. **Encouragement:** Just like clearing the physical space makes it easier to find things, so does sorting and organizing your flip-flops makes decision-making much easier when preparing for summer events.

Creative Repurposing

This process of eliminating clutter from one's environment does not imply that everything gets thrown into the bin. It is possible to turn old flip-flops into new and even interesting items and accessories with the help of creativity. They can be converted into garden planters, weird coasters, or other similar something that lends a peculiarity to your homes. Such projects are not only eco-friendly but also represent a great chance to be as creative as you would like and make whatever you need with your own hands. **Hint:** Some ideas on family involvement include; assembling all the necessary items to create a craft summer day. **Guidance:** It is also important that you take your time on the internet to look at ideas and procedures on how you can transform your flip-flops. **Encouragement:** Therefore, instead of discarding the items and replacing them with new ones you are engulfing yourself in a sustainable culture and getting a product of your own in the process.

Embracing Minimalism

Organizing the flip-flops needed for the summer is not just a form of tidying up – it's defining a lifestyle of less is more. By so doing, a person can consider every object they possess worthwhile and worthy of having the personal touch. Simple living not only makes you lose the burden but also gives you comfort and a clear lifestyle to proceed with your life. **Prompt:** Reflect and ponder over the question "How do I relate to this item in the present?" Furthermore, understand that simplicity brings joy – do not focus on anything more than what makes you happy. **Encouragement:** To cite an instance, you start decluttering your house, and you will realize that there is space for you, and your family to enjoy the summer and the things that matter most in life.

Autumn Decluttering: Preparing for Cozy and Clutter-Free Spaces

Introduction to Autumn Decluttering

As the weather starts getting cooler, and the trees shedding its leaves, it is the best time to get the house ready for the enclosed evenings with a beautiful fireplace. Autumn decluttering is, to a greater extent, about designing an environment that is conducive to the creation of warmth and coziness. In the process of decluttering, you free space for the things that should be present – leisure and peace. Here are the best five reasons why it is important for you too to transition from spring cleaning to autumn cleaning: **Hint:** To anyone I imagine spending an evening on a couch in a clean and tidy living room while reading a book and the lights are dim with the lights of autumn around. **Guidance:** Begin with choosing a free space in your house that, in your opinion, can use additional attention and care, for example, the living room or the bedroom. **Encouragement:** Approach this task with the goal in mind that removing those items brings you one step closer to having that warm and cozy home for the chilly seasons.

Wardrobe Transition

As you know, warm days are coming to an end hence the need to change your outfit from summer wear to autumn wear. Start by changing the position of clothes, storing warmer pulling out heavier clothes, and putting away summer clothes. Go through each item that was purchased during summer and determine if it is worth keeping or throwing away or even if it should be donated. This is also a good time to tidy items commonly worn during the autumn making sure that you can access them easily. **Prompt:** A good rule of thumb is to ask yourself "When was the last time I wore this?" If you haven't used the item for several months, then it is the perfect time to let it go. **Guidance:** Consider this shift a chance to declutter all your clothes and have only the best and most oft-worn pieces. **Encouragement:** Just think how comfortable each morning would be if your closet is clean and you have only the right sizes and clothes that you feel best wearing with the onset of the crisp autumn weather.

Living Room Transformation

Winter is the time to make your rooms warm and comfortable and make your body and soul feel comfortable too. Move to your illustration – living room: clear up space for comfort. All non-essentials should be put away or discarded so as not to distort the feel of the nice interior. Next, it is necessary to incorporate the factors that make the preparation of the room more comfortable, including warm beds, light, and soft pillows. Things such as autumnal wreaths or candles can help bring ambiance while at the same time helping in avoiding clutter. **Hint:** You should be able to imagine that when you are coming into the living room there is the feel of the cold outside and the living room is everything warm and comfortable. **Guidance:** Coordination with the current décor of the house and look for ornaments that depict the theme of the season subtly. **Encouragement:** However, remember that a neat and clean living room is as welcoming as cozy, and therefore, during autumn you want to enjoy its warm colors as much as possible.

Kitchen and Pantry Refresh

When autumn comes it is high time to update the kitchen and pantry to fit the specific needs and culinary trends of the new season. Begin to survey the household pantry, time it, and ask everyone in the household to discard expired foods. It enables you to arrange your items on the shelves for autumn use such as spices, soups, and baking products which could be easily retrieved when required. That is why it is important to keep the kitchen clean and tidy, thanks to its organization, meal preparation is fun and not tiresome. **Prompt:** The one question you need to ask yourself is, "Do I still need this item, is it still useful to me this season?" If the answer is a negative then it is time to let the item go.

Guidance: One key aspect of organizing is compartmentalizing the items that are used regularly so that they can be easily retrieved – In this case, group similar items together, and store them in appropriately labeled clear containers.

Encouragement: A neatly laid kitchen saves so much time apart from creating an atmosphere for those warm home-cooked meals ideal for the cool autumns.

Day 20-21:
Set Up a Dedicated Decluttering Space

Steps to Create Your Decluttering Space	Check
Choose a spacious, well-lit area in your home	[ ]
Clear the area of any distractions or unrelated items	[ ]
Set up tables or surfaces for sorting items into categories	[ ]
Arrange boxes or bins for "Donate," "Recycle," "Trash," and "Keep"	[ ]
Prepare a space for items that need to be relocated or repaired	[ ]
Ensure the space is comfortable, with adequate seating and ventilation	[ ]
Keep all your decluttering supplies within easy reach	[ ]
Play calming music to create a relaxing atmosphere	[ ]
Have refreshments nearby to stay hydrated and energized	[ ]
Create a checklist to track your progress during each session	[ ]

Organizing Items by Categories	Check
Donate: Items in good condition that no longer serve you but could benefit others	[ ]
Recycle: Items that can be repurposed or recycled instead of discarded	[ ]
Trash: Broken, expired, or unusable items that must be discarded	[ ]
Keep: Useful Items, bring joy, and align with your minimalist goals	[ ]
Relocate: Items that belong in another room or space	[ ]
Repair: Items that need fixing before they can be used or donated	[ ]
Sell: Items that are valuable and could be sold instead of donated	[ ]

Action	Check
Set up your dedicated decluttering space to facilitate an organized process	[ ]
Sort items into the appropriate categories as you go	[ ]
Keep your decluttering space clean and organized throughout the process	[ ]
Track your progress by updating your checklist regularly	[ ]
Reflect on the sense of accomplishment as your space becomes more organized	[ ]

Winter Decluttering: Creating a Warm and Welcoming Home

Introduction to Winter Decluttering

With the onset of winter colder weather, it is the best time to begin decluttering your home for the season. The purpose is to design the room to be cozy, and comfortable so that you can escape the cold of winter. It means that decluttering now will allow you to pay attention to what is important – warmth and comfort. **Hint:** Ideally, it is like returning home during winter from the cold and the house enveloping you in warmth; that is what you stand to get from winter decluttering. **Guidance:** First of all, it is necessary to define zones that are most likely to become messy, like the porch, the living room, and so on, and then concentrate on creating comfort. **Encouragement:** As a reminder, getting ready for winter is not just about aesthetics but about creating an atmosphere in which you can be happy and cozy during this time.

Holiday Decluttering

During the festive period, there is joy, and with joy comes plenty of decorations, presents, and parties. Begin by conducting holiday season organization and removing unnecessary items from your home. Discard all of the items that you do not use or have minimal use for – put the remaining items in bins with clear labels for convenience's sake. The next step is organizing the gifts where gift-wrap management is followed by de-cluttering the gift wraps and planning for the gift storing too. Lastly, tidy your entertaining spaces and this refers to those areas of the home where people will be gathered to have fun and in the process eliminate all signs of clutter. **Prompt:** One has to ask themselves, does this decoration spark joy, if it does not, one may have to leave it with the charity. **Guidance:** When decorating for the holidays, do not overdo it, use items that bring out the true meaning of the occasion. **Encouragement:** In this manner, you will minimize stress about your home environment before the holidays set in, and in turn have a clean and warm setting that will enable you to appreciate the company of friends and family.

Bedroom Comfort

Winter is all about having a great night's sleep in a warm and comfy bed, the organization of bedroom space should be done well to eliminate interference. To warm up the bedroom, start with your beddings; change your light-weighted ones and pull out your warm, dark, and heavy ones or your flannel sheets. Prepare your winter clothes so that all your garments can be easily found and stored in a clean and tidy manner. A tidied-up room contributes significantly to good sleep and particularly in these cold seasons, the room feels like a den from the cold. **Hint:** Your bedroom should be your space where you wane in during cold winter and feel comfortable to stay there. **Guidance:** For instance, it will be nice to have your summer clothes and bedding packed and stored in bins labeled summer so that you create space for your winter items. **Encouragement:** A neat bedroom is your comfort zone from the frost – it's an area where one can warm up during the long winter nights.

Eco-Friendly Practices

Reducing clutter during the winter season is the ideal chance of embracing environmental conservation. As a rule, separate what you can give away or sell, and convert it into a donation or recyclable product, not a piece of trash. Ensure that the concepts of reuse and recycling form the basis of all your projects of cleaning and eliminating clutter from your home. The objective is to keep the house always clean to avoid clutter, and at the same time, to reduce the negative impact on the environment. **Prompt:** "What should I do with this item so that it does not harm the environment?" **Guidance:** One of the things that people should do is look for non-profit organizations that collect and donate items that are still useful. **Encouragement:** In essence, for you to gain just and effective strategies for decluttering it is advisable that you only select those that will result in a cleaner environment for future generations.

Conclusion

Recap of Seasonal Benefits: It is advised to declutter throughout the year but each season has some advantages for it. Spring is a good time to work on something fresh and new, lightness is encouraged in the summer, cozier feelings in autumn, and warmth in winter. Decluttering with the seasons means that you arrange the areas by the natural and personal cycles, which improves your welfare.

Embracing Change: Welcome all four seasons in a calendar year as useful tools for tidying up and cleaning up your home. Such changes as changing clothes for different times of the year, redecorating the living room, or preparing your kitchen for different types of meals are on different levels assisting in keeping you organized and always in tune with what is current. Encouragement: The approach to areas of the house clutter typically overcomes the difficulties associated with periods of decluttering to bring you closer to having the home you need all year round.

Looking Forward: As you expect each coming season, expect the pleasure of being in a clean house, uncluttered, free from unwanted things that do not add value to your life. An organization that is created in your work area makes your environment easy to manage and also enables a person to live a less stressful life. Hint: Just think about the idea of walking into every season in a year with a home that will be ready to provide support to all your activities.

Chapter 7: Stay Passionate

The Heart vs. the Home: Finding Balance

Introduction to Emotional Decluttering

Decluttering invariably becomes an internal tug-of-war between a sentimental heart and a cluttered home. While such possessions are important as they bring back memories, they are usually in contradistinctive associated with clutter which interferes with the order in your home. Hence, it is important to gain control of such feelings, and alongside them, fulfill more functional concerns to obtain a tidy home. First of all, it is quite natural to have some emotional bond with material things, however, it is equally important to understand that it is possible to design a living environment that will help you find harmony. **Hint:** Consider making your home free of unnecessary distractions and it's free of clutter, only the most important and sentimental items are left. **Guidance:** Emotional decluttering, therefore, needs to be done out of compassion because it is the decision to let go of the past to create room for the future. **Encouragement:** As I've stressed before, let me repeat it once again: organizing does not equal forgetting, it equals remembering healthily and efficiently.

Understanding Sentimental Attachments

For some reason, sentimental items seem capable of reproducing and occupying as much space as possible without much intervention on your part. They are the 'Sentimental Multiplier Effect' in which anything appears to personify a memory or even an anecdote thereby becoming hard to let go.

Approaching this in Digital Memory Books is one way to do this. Thus, instead of bringing those things into your room, which can add to the mess, at least by capturing pictures of them, you can keep the memories more efficiently. **Prompt:** Think to yourself, "What this item reminds me of, and is it possible to preserve it without this thing?" Advice: Use a few things and find out that often the memory is as vivid as if the thing is with you. **Encouragement:** After some time you will only be happy that you are in a simple environment free from clutter and can at the same time cherish memories of the past.

Kid-Friendly Decluttering

Clutter arises easily in children's work areas, for focusing on a formal tidy-up was particularly difficult. Yet, it is possible to encourage kids to declutter by gamifying the process, it is not a sin to be positive. It also avoids associating cleaning up as a chore, thus, fun activities such as treasure hunts or making clutter monster boxes make tidying up fun. **Hint:** Using a timer, let your kids search for as many 'treasures,' or toys they have not used in a long while, as they can in the period that is given to them. **Guidance:** They should be encouraged by motivational items like dancing or having a bar of their favorite food once the cleaning is done. **Encouragement:** This also makes decluttering a fun activity that must be done and on top of that, it becomes a learning session for your children on the importance of having a clean and well-arranged place.

Digital Decluttering

With technology today, it is not so uncommon to have devices filled with files, pictures, and emails. Having a day dedicated to Tech Detox will do you a lot of good as you go through the day organizing your technological life. Organizing one's docs, going through the photos, and decluttering email inbox would be a good start. **Prompt:** Question yourself, if you need to store the file or not. **Advice:** Make sections within the folders for the documents and dispose of the ones you do not need anymore. **Encouragement:** When you begin removing items from your digital world, one of those things you are bound to see is exactly how much your productivity rate rises and how good you will start to feel. A clean digital space does mean a clean mind, one that can help to filter out the noise to concentrate on the important.

Day 22:
Focus on the Kitchen

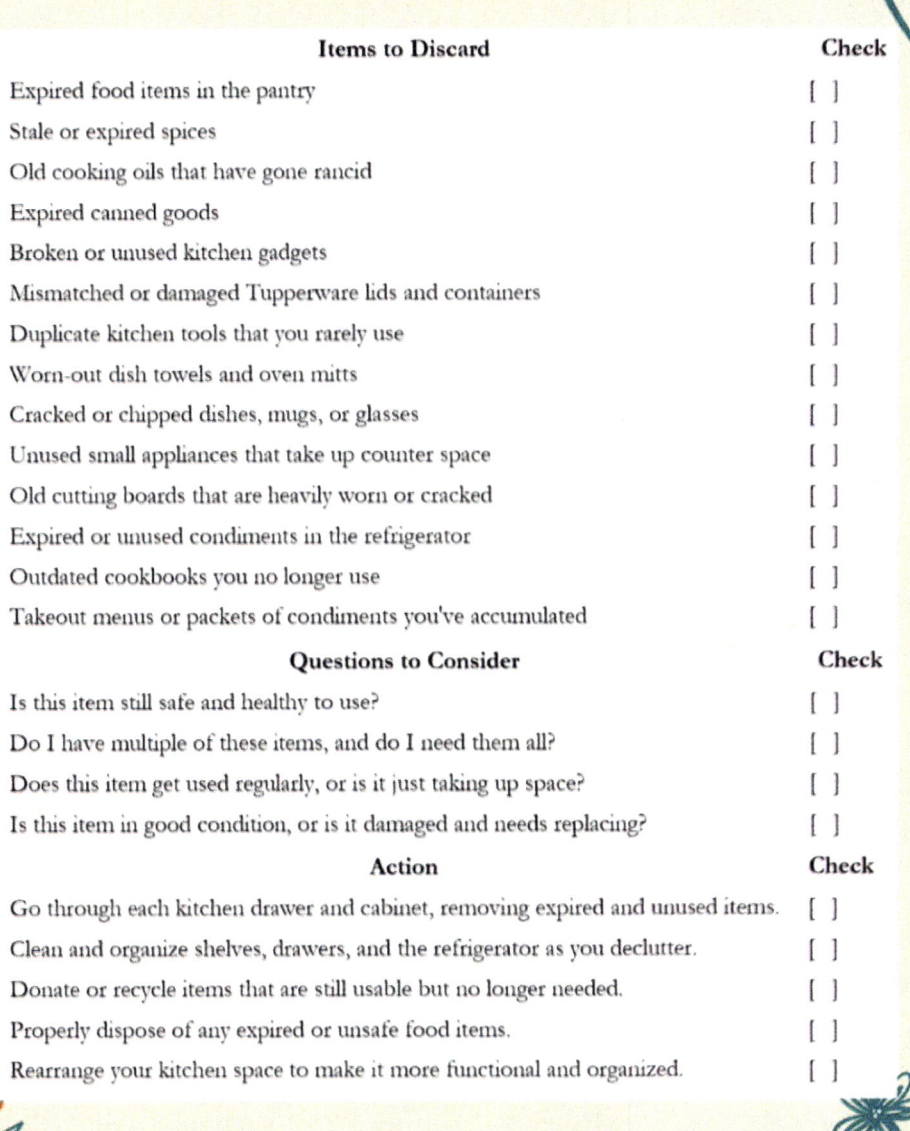

Items to Discard	Check
Expired food items in the pantry	[ ]
Stale or expired spices	[ ]
Old cooking oils that have gone rancid	[ ]
Expired canned goods	[ ]
Broken or unused kitchen gadgets	[ ]
Mismatched or damaged Tupperware lids and containers	[ ]
Duplicate kitchen tools that you rarely use	[ ]
Worn-out dish towels and oven mitts	[ ]
Cracked or chipped dishes, mugs, or glasses	[ ]
Unused small appliances that take up counter space	[ ]
Old cutting boards that are heavily worn or cracked	[ ]
Expired or unused condiments in the refrigerator	[ ]
Outdated cookbooks you no longer use	[ ]
Takeout menus or packets of condiments you've accumulated	[ ]

Questions to Consider	Check
Is this item still safe and healthy to use?	[ ]
Do I have multiple of these items, and do I need them all?	[ ]
Does this item get used regularly, or is it just taking up space?	[ ]
Is this item in good condition, or is it damaged and needs replacing?	[ ]

Action	Check
Go through each kitchen drawer and cabinet, removing expired and unused items.	[ ]
Clean and organize shelves, drawers, and the refrigerator as you declutter.	[ ]
Donate or recycle items that are still usable but no longer needed.	[ ]
Properly dispose of any expired or unsafe food items.	[ ]
Rearrange your kitchen space to make it more functional and organized.	[ ]

Creating a Memory Box: Where Sentimental Items Go to Retire

Choosing the Right Container

When organizing personal belongings, the container you use should be unique, and the atmosphere inside must be welcoming and inspiring for your precious treasures. Regardless, it can be an old suitcase, a storage chest that will be decorated, or a wooden box made by your hands, choose an item that will suit you and your home. **Hint:** A personal memory box should be seen as a repository for one's history, which doesn't have to exist actively within an individual's experience. **Guidance:** Make sure the box is strong and big enough to contain what you wish to store. **Encouragement:** When picking a gorgeous and significant vessel, one is not merely placing objects to be kept; instead, one designs a special place for the memories to be treasured.

Curating Your Collection

Picking what goes inside the memory box demands some crucial questions that one should answer. Is this item cheerful? Is it in some way special to me? If not, it might be time to let it go – such is a powerful motto to grab if you want to proceed with the powerful idea. This process makes you let go of things that are not very close to your heart, thus enabling you to concentrate on the ones that matter most to you. **Prompt:** Try to ask yourself a question, "If this item is not here, would I miss it?" The only thing we need to consider is whether the feeling that we have inside when an item is missing is a positive one. **Encouragement:** To throw away something that one uses no more may be one of the most transformative actions leading to the organization of a home that speaks of the occupant's present life.

Labeling and Organizing

For one to effectively practice memory boxes, some Measures must be put in place aimed at protecting the memory box thus setting boundaries is vital. Sticker the container so that other people will not interfere with its contents and also so that you will remember what the box is meant for. Labels also assist in reminding one what is inside the box and also in maintaining the order of the items in the box. **Hint:** It is possible to label it based on the memories it contains for instance, "Family Holidays" or "Childhood Treasures". Periodically, ensure that the box is in the proper order and that the additional items being placed in the box are done so in an orderly manner. **Encouragement:** It therefore only makes sense that labeling and organizing your memory box assists you in your ability to bring your past into your present without it dominating all that is current, making it easier for one to enjoy memories without fussing with every little thing.

Revisiting the Memory Box

A memory box can be opened after some time so that one can see whether the things put in the box are worth keeping. This practice ensures that the box does not disintegrate into a storage box for all the unnecessary items that one gathers in a day, week, or month. **Prompt:** It is also important to remind a patient to open the memory box every six months or if there is any other major change in their life. **Guidance:** As you pass through the box, wonder whether you still relate to each of them. If not, then, it is okay to let it go. **Encouragement:** It is a way to appreciate the history and the past, but it is still not letting it get in the way of the present life by restarting the clutter invasion in the home.

Day 23:

Tackle the Bathroom

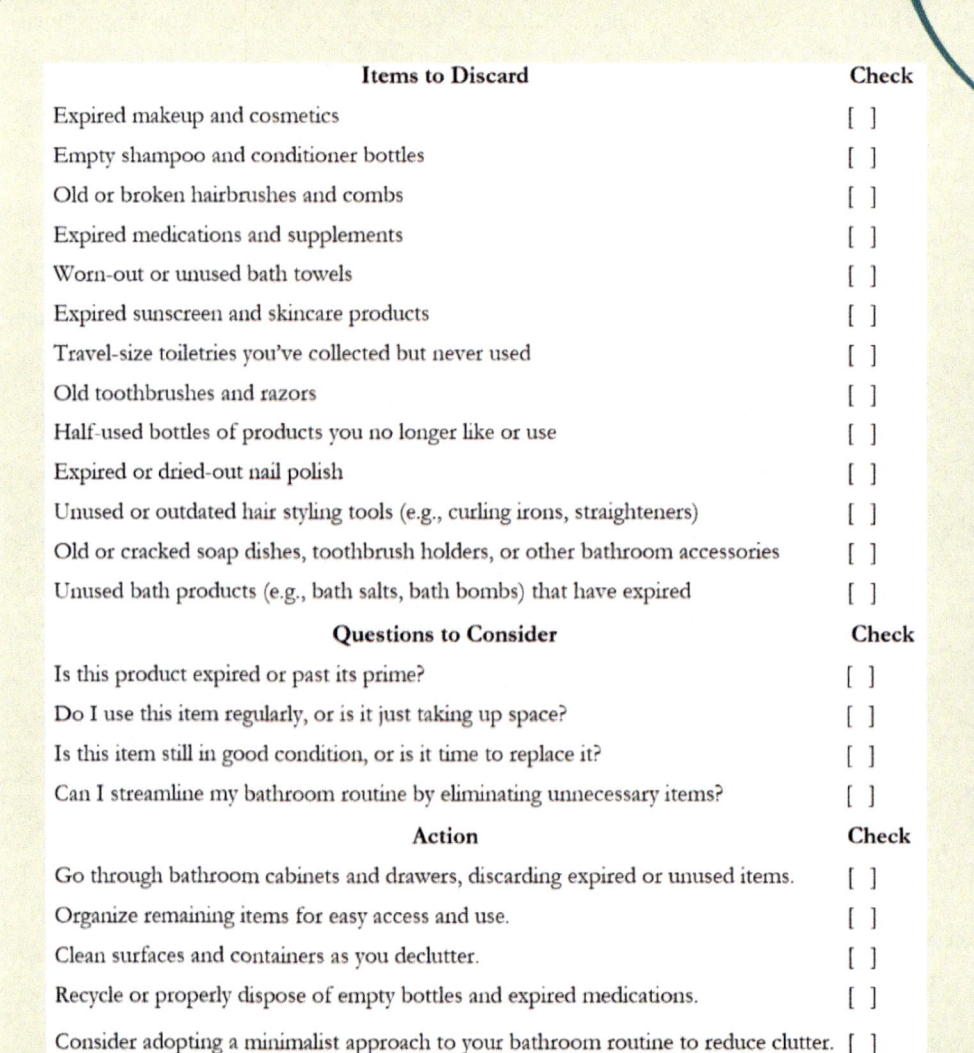

Items to Discard	Check
Expired makeup and cosmetics	[ ]
Empty shampoo and conditioner bottles	[ ]
Old or broken hairbrushes and combs	[ ]
Expired medications and supplements	[ ]
Worn-out or unused bath towels	[ ]
Expired sunscreen and skincare products	[ ]
Travel-size toiletries you've collected but never used	[ ]
Old toothbrushes and razors	[ ]
Half-used bottles of products you no longer like or use	[ ]
Expired or dried-out nail polish	[ ]
Unused or outdated hair styling tools (e.g., curling irons, straighteners)	[ ]
Old or cracked soap dishes, toothbrush holders, or other bathroom accessories	[ ]
Unused bath products (e.g., bath salts, bath bombs) that have expired	[ ]

Questions to Consider	Check
Is this product expired or past its prime?	[ ]
Do I use this item regularly, or is it just taking up space?	[ ]
Is this item still in good condition, or is it time to replace it?	[ ]
Can I streamline my bathroom routine by eliminating unnecessary items?	[ ]

Action	Check
Go through bathroom cabinets and drawers, discarding expired or unused items.	[ ]
Organize remaining items for easy access and use.	[ ]
Clean surfaces and containers as you declutter.	[ ]
Recycle or properly dispose of empty bottles and expired medications.	[ ]
Consider adopting a minimalist approach to your bathroom routine to reduce clutter.	[ ]

Seasonal Decluttering

Spring Cleaning

Spring is associated with renewal and therefore is the most appropriate time to engage in a complete spring cleaning of your house. Applying the Marie Kondo method during this period would be good since it allows one to approach the items freshly. Center on objects such as closets since they're spaces that eventually become full of items one rarely thinks about. When deciding whether to keep an item or not, you are encouraged to ask yourself, 'Does this item bring me joy? Chasing away winter does not only mean cleaning our houses and getting rid of dust; it also brings changes in our character. **Hint:** Try to consider decluttering as a process of preparing for the new season, when it is time to leave behind clutter and welcome fresh opportunities. **Guidance:** It should therefore be taken gradually and every stage should not be rushed through. **Encouragement:** Welcome new energy associated with spring and be open for it to transform both your home and you as an individual.

Autumn Decluttering

Since the holidays are just around the corner in the autumn, it will be useful to start cleaning the house and stocking it for the winter. Begin by accessing toys decorations and other items that may have been collected throughout the year. This creates space for new gifts and also keeps the compound tidy throughout the festive period. Autumn also symbolizes the change in the sense of transition in the natural cycle, as well as a transition in one's life. This should be perhaps the best time to review what is required and what lies in store during the winter months. **Prompt:** Reflect on what you need to remove to create a space for holiday happiness. **Advice:** Concentrate on closets and shared living areas that are most frequently used during the holidays. Encouragement: Regular decluttering also ensures you have a clean home to start the holiday and make the seasons enjoyable for everyone.

Winter Cozy-Up

Winter is a time of hot atmosphere and warmth, so it is the perfect time to pay attention to the creation of comfortable and welcoming interiors in your home. Where to begin? Try organizing the primary spaces such as the living room for those who sit in front of the fire during the chillier months. Whereas cluttering interferes with the optimal creation of ample space, possessing less clutter makes it possible to create an inviting and comfortable atmosphere of space. Go for sparseness and get rid of the things that clutter space, but do keep things in your room that are necessities like soft blankets, warm lights, and other essentials that you might want to have around you. **Hint:** Imagine your home as a winter shelter—what items can be taken away to make the atmosphere warmer? **Guidance:** The emphasis should be on making the place not only aesthetically pleasant but also inviting. **Encouragement:** Clean and comfortable surroundings in the house will be warm in winter, and will create a comfortable space to spend the day inside.

Summer Simplification

Everyone's wish to have a lighter and easier life should be accorded in the summer hence the need to simplify one's living space. Cleaning during this time would also make the surroundings free from congestion hence making the rooms look more enjoyable. Concentrate on the decreasing of load, that is on taking out things that are heavy and could be useless in your home. Also, the activities and some specific structures such as outside space are more appropriate during summer. Get rid of clutter and unnecessary things, especially inside the home, and spend as much time out in the open air, to feel the essence of the season. **Prompt:** Self-Quiz: How can I make my home feel as light as the summer breeze? **Help:** The best idea is to pay special attention to the openness of the zones, such as the kitchen and living room. **Encouragement:** When you declutter your space, one of the best compliments you build upon is that of summer and, by doing so, turn your home into a summer house proper.

Practical Tips and Encouragements for Emotional Decluttering

Starting Small

With emotional decluttering, it is often wise to start small so that you do not get overwhelmed. Start with one drawer, one shelf, or even a small box of objects that you have been for some time that you wanted to arrange. The idea is to concentrate on areas within one's control and where results are easy to quantify. People should bear in mind though that decluttering is not about achieving the perfect state; it is all about creating progress. This is true because every single move is made nearer to the ultimate goal of having a light and serene environment free from clutter. **Hint:** Begin with one section or compartment and if successful give yourself a pat on the back. **Guidance:** Spend 15 minutes every day tidying up this or that area and grow to the complete day of tidying up. **Encouragement:** They also understand that practice makes perfect and hence it is better to progress than to be perfect. This way, you will slowly and gradually get used to it and get to see the positive effects of decluttering without experiencing annoyance.

Sentimental Item Alternatives

It can be hard to part with sentimental items but one does not necessarily have to throw them away or get rid of them; there are ways how one can still cherish such items and not produce clutter. Take digital pictures of such items which you do not want to part with but you have to part with them. Another form of rage against the loss of sentimental objects is to transform them into artistic productions, as in making a quilt into a wall hanging or putting a piece of a favorite childhood dress into a frame. **Prompt:** Say to yourself, "How could I pay this memory a new respect?" **Advice:** Consider the sentimental value of the object, rather than the actual item. **Encouragement:** Through the innovative methods of preserving the items that hold our sentimental values, then you can eliminate this clutter while still having your memories within arms' reach.

Family Involvement

Involving family members to participate in the cleaning process is less hard and also provides a chance to share and archive important memories. Make each family member participate in the process by making them go through all their belongings, to be grouped into those to be kept back, donated, or disposed of. This is a good opportunity to narrate and discuss the past events, and happenings. Besides, consider using decluttering as an opportunity to start new traditions for the family like the annual donation or the memory evening. **Prompt:** Discuss with your family members 3 questions: What memories does this item evoke? Decluttering should be a fun process where all the members of the family get to contribute. **Encouragement:** Coordination ensures that you make your home neater while on the same note, you bond with your family and make good memories.

Maintaining Momentum

In decluttering, sustainability is crucial; that is why one should stay active in the process for a long time. It is important also to have time for house cleaning when you are planning to declutter and organize your house. Be it a weekly clean-up of the house or a quarterly cleaning spree; it has to be done regularly.

It is important to remember to party along the way too, for instance after you are through with a large cleaning exercise or whenever you achieve an objective. **Hint:** It is also important to start a decluttering journal where one can write down a personal experience that is in the process of the decluttering process with the ability to being able to look back on how far one has come. **Guidance:** Check specific zones of the house that always get messy and work on them before they become out of hand. **Encouragement:** Take pride in the accomplishment no matter how small, this way, you will be encouraged that every disposed of item should be thrown, donated, or sold, whichever is appropriate, and proper disposition of such items is vital As you embark on a decluttering process, you should always bear in mind that every victory counts.

Day 24-25:

Declutter Your Bedroom

Items to Discard	Check
Expired makeup and cosmetics	[ ]
Empty shampoo and conditioner bottles	[ ]
Old or broken hairbrushes and combs	[ ]
Expired medications and supplements	[ ]
Worn-out or unused bath towels	[ ]
Expired sunscreen and skincare products	[ ]
Travel-size toiletries you've collected but never used	[ ]
Old toothbrushes and razors	[ ]
Half-used bottles of products you no longer like or use	[ ]
Expired or dried-out nail polish	[ ]
Unused or outdated hair styling tools (e.g., curling irons, straighteners)	[ ]
Old or cracked soap dishes, toothbrush holders, or other bathroom accessories	[ ]
Unused bath products (e.g., bath salts, bath bombs) that have expired	[ ]

Questions to Consider	Check
Is this product expired or past its prime?	[ ]
Do I use this item regularly, or is it just taking up space?	[ ]
Is this item still in good condition, or is it time to replace it?	[ ]
Can I streamline my bathroom routine by eliminating unnecessary items?	[ ]

Action	Check
Go through bathroom cabinets and drawers, discarding expired or unused items.	[ ]
Organize remaining items for easy access and use.	[ ]
Clean surfaces and containers as you declutter.	[ ]
Recycle or properly dispose of empty bottles and expired medications.	[ ]
Consider adopting a minimalist approach to your bathroom routine to reduce clutter.	[ ]

Conclusion

Recap of Emotional Decluttering Benefits: Cluttering is not just a physical process but a mental state as well, emotional decluttering provides deep impacts on sanity. Selling saved tickets means reduced clutter and, therefore, reduced stress because your mind is not weighed down by things that you do not use anymore. Clutter in particular brings disorder into the house and makes it hard for a person to concentrate on matters of importance. This process also benefits one's mood and helps one become more oriented in the environment, giving a sense of control. Guidance: Indeed consider how you have benefited from the aspect of emotional decluttering to enhance your general well-being.

Embracing the Journey: Tidying up is a process that is worth starting because it entails determination, laughter, and tolerance. I mean, it is a process and it is okay to watch the process with a light heart knowing that some things should take as they are but as they are slowly transforming. Make a joke out of it, cherish all the moments you overcome a hurdle in the process of letting go, and remember that it is perfectly okay to be your support system. Hint: Remember that even the smallest of the advances is an advance nonetheless. Guidance: Approach each stage with the realization that the challenges make for a better life, and one that is minus the anxiety of life. Encouragement: If you treat the process as a journey and laugh at yourself when you hesitate in making your decision, you will find that it is not punishment but a joy to get rid of everything you no longer need.

Looking Forward: Depending on how far you have gone in your decluttering process, always look forward to the improvement of the quality of your life. For instance, a neat environment at home leads to the elimination of physical barriers that are associated with clutter, thereby encouraging new opportunities, relationships, and experiences in homes. It lets you exist in a manner that is much more deliberate, with time for the important things. Prompt: Another part of decluttering questions is "What new opportunities will arise when I remove the clutter?" Even though each next step will make your life more ordered, try to concentrate on the results, as this is the way you're moving towards a better life. Encouragement: Cleaning up is all about reclaiming your space and starting anew and so should be entered into with happiness and excitement.

Chapter 8: Eco-Friendly Decluttering: Sustainable Practices for Disposing of Unwanted Items

The Three Rs: Reduce, Reuse, Recycle (and Resist the Urge to Hoard)

Introduction to the Three Rs

The underlying principle of the green approach to decluttering is expressed in the Three Rs: Reduce, Reuse, and Recycle. Declutter your house to free space and your mind as well. Less accumulation makes it easier to organize, dust, and pack away, thus, only keeping the important things. Recycling may be all about creativity—how do you use an object again instead of throwing it away? A glass jar can easily be stylish storage and old clothes can become cleaning cloths. Re-use wherever possible, re-processing used material into new products to reduce the amount of waste produced. Finally, there is the ability to name the desire to hoard by embracing and resisting hoarding. **Hint:** One should ask themselves whether the particular item has any positive contribution to their life and if it does not, then it has to be discarded. **Encouragement:** I can put on record that the incorporation of the three Rs as a way of life is not only effective in easing your life but is a key step in making the entire world green.

Reducing Clutter

To start the process of excessive accumulation of things, and to achieve a more successful and orderly living space, it is necessary to clear and minimize clutter. Start Small as you can tackle just one room at a time for instance, instead of focusing on everything at once, you can focus on let's enhance this room only. Start with a drawer, one shelf, or, at best, a corner of a room. Such an approach makes the task more easy to handle and creates the groundwork for larger assignments. The principle of Mindful Reduction is to sort through one's belongings and only retain what gives joy or is utilitarian. When you reach an item, you should always ask yourself if you have a special affection for it or if you have used it recently, if not then it is time to discard it. Cleanliness also implies lightening the mental burden associated with clutter, which is what is meant by the term Mental Load. Of course, there are fewer things to worry about and fewer things that could clutter up a person's life and prevent them from enjoying the important things and fulfilling them. **Encouragement:** Each thing that you let go of is a move towards living a life that is stress-free and free of clutter.

Reusing Items

Recycling is not only good for the environment but can also serve as an interesting solution when it comes to designing homes. Creative Repurposing means that worn-out clothes can be used for cleaning or jars for storage. What composes this approach is that it not only constitutes economic benefits but also minimizes the frequency of purchasing materials. Do home decorating Projects that involve the reuse of furniture or other items into trendy chic furniture. Further, an old wardrobe may be repainted and rejacketed to become a trendy wardrobe. One can also use the concept in some cases and give items a Second Chance by changing their specialties. An old ladder turns into a kind of bookshelf; a suitcase would add an antique feel as a coffee table. **Hint:** Walking by any item in your home, ask, How can I make this look new? **Encouragement:** reusing saves on the environment while at the same time providing a way of coming up with unique pieces that are one of a kind.

Recycling Practices

Proper recycling is a key component of eco-friendly decluttering. Knowledge of what can be recycled and accurate recycling methods is important. Proper Recycling includes sorting items into paper, glass, plastic, and Electronics according to the Recycling Regulations of the region. This helps in making sure that they undergo the required processes and then convert for use that is needed. Participate in self-recycling projects that involve recycling of material, for instance by melting old candle wax into new candles or using bottle tops to create masterpieces This way they feel that they have contributed by recycling, as well as get a sense of achievement. Recycling may also be utilized as the next step in the model in that it can be an Emotional Cleansing. Next time when you are reusing some material item, try and picture yourself 'opening a new box of energy' filled with positive emotions and casting away all the negativity. **Guidance:** Before recycling, one should ask him or herself, "Can this item be used for something else?" **Motivation:** Every recycled item these days brings the world closer to a better environment and helps lead a lighter, healthier life.

Resisting the Urge to Hoard

A major challenge to decluttering is hoarding but once the issues causing it are identified one can effectively deal with it. Hoarding Triggers are known by understanding why you feel compelled to retain specific things. What is it that individuals perceive in such transactions – is it the romantic notion of the object, fear of throwing something away, or security? Once they've been labeled, it is much simpler to dispute them. Questions such as 'Will I need to use this again?' or 'This item is just occupying space, doesn't it?' are some of the questions which may assist you decide on whether to retain the item or not. Remember, that Living Space vs. Museum – Your home must be comfortable and practical not an antique depot. **Hint:** Think about the happiness that comes with cleanliness and having a neat environment compared to the momentary relief that comes with your clutter. **Encouragement:** A clean home does not hold things that are not necessary to create a serene environment.

Day 26-28:
Move to Living Areas and Home Office

Living Areas—Items to Discard	Check
Old magazines, newspapers, or catalogs	[ ]
DVDs, CDs, or video games you no longer use	[ ]
Old remote controls or electronics that no longer work	[ ]
Outdated or damaged decor items	[ ]
Extra blankets, throws, or pillows that are worn out or never used	[ ]
Unused or broken picture frames	[ ]
Burnt-out candles or candle holders	[ ]
Books you've read and don't plan to reread	[ ]
Board games or puzzles with missing pieces	[ ]
Old or broken furniture that takes up space	[ ]

Home Office—Items to Discard	Check
Old papers, receipts, or bills that you no longer need	[ ]
Broken or outdated electronics (e.g., old phones, printers)	[ ]
Pens that have run out of ink	[ ]
Empty notebooks or pads that are no longer usable	[ ]
Business cards or contact information you no longer need	[ ]
Outdated office supplies or equipment	[ ]
Unused or outdated files, folders, or binders	[ ]
Manuals or guides for items you no longer own	[ ]
Expired coupons, flyers, or promotional materials	[ ]
Old calendars or planners	[ ]

Questions to Consider	Check
Does this item still serve a purpose in my living area or office?	[ ]
Am I holding onto this item out of habit rather than necessity?	[ ]
Is this item taking up space that could be used more effectively?	[ ]
Can I digitize this item instead of keeping a physical copy?	[ ]

Action	Check
Go through each living area and office space, discarding unused or outdated items	[ ]
Organize your books, electronics, and decor for a clutter-free environment	[ ]
Streamline your home office by digitizing files and organizing supplies	[ ]
Donate or recycle items that are still usable but no longer needed	[ ]
Set up a system to maintain a clutter-free living area and office	[ ]

Creative Ways to Donate and Recycle: Giving Your Stuff a Second Life

Donating Items

Giving away the items is one of the most effective ways of getting rid of the clutter and being helpful to others at the same time. Sorting and Relocating: Friends can be persuaded to participate in a Donate-a-thon Party where you sort out what you need to keep and what is necessary to donate. This is relatively easier to accomplish when making it a communal process; it is not so tiresome and seems more fun. Find local Charity and Thrift Stores and determine if they accept donations and if you are aware of their regulations so as not to waste your items. Not only does donating support the war effort to clear your space but contributes to the Community Impact to help those in need. **Guidance:** Questions to ask yourself: Before donating, ask yourself, "Could this item bring value to someone else's life?" **Encouragement:** Every item you donate is a gift to someone else and it brings you one step closer to the minimalist lifestyle.

Upcycling Projects

Upcycling means repurposing an item and giving it a new and fashionable look. Thinking about giving Furniture Makeovers a try—a can of paint, and updated knobs, and screws can transform an old dresser into a new one. Likewise, Clothing Repurposing is versatile to infinity – for instance, they can transform old jeans into tote bags or patchwork quilts. Crafting Ideas lets you repurpose materials for DIY home improvements; they give your house character; they are resourceful. For instance, when redecorating, refurbishing wooden pallets is wise for new shelves, or old frames that can be used to hang newly bought paintings. **Hint:** Try to ask yourself one question: "How can I give a new life to this object?" **Guidance:** upcycling does not only mean transforming the product into a new object but also helping the world become even a little bit greener. **Encouragement:** Every piece upcycled is a declaration of how you are willing to protect the environment and embrace new ideas and ways of doing things without a trace of clutter.

Item Swapping

In item swapping, you and the other participants get rid of clutters in a manner that is both sustainable and can foster community. Open for friends and neighbors to exchange items they no longer have a use for, Hosting Swap Meets helps get items into the hands that will give them a new lease on life. Set Basic Guidelines again in the same vain to prevent a tendency of more cluttering to one person than the other only exchange items that are clean and only make sure that everyone takes fewer things than they brought. Apart from recycling, this leads to the fostering of connections and an amplified sense of Community Building, thereby being an effective practice. **Prompt:** Contemplation Guide: Before engaging in the swap meet, participants should ask themselves, "Is there someone in my community who could use this?" Share with the students several reasons why the swap meet is preferable to buying something new. **Encouragement:** Item swapping is not just about reducing clutter; it's about creating a sense of community and collective responsibility toward a sustainable future.

Day 29: Revisit Your Progress

Areas to Revisit	Check
Kitchen: Double-check for any remaining expired food or unused gadgets.	[ ]
Bathroom: Ensure all expired products and empty containers have been discarded.	[ ]
Bedroom: Confirm that all worn-out clothes, shoes, and accessories have been addressed.	[ ]
Living Areas: Revisit bookshelves, electronics, and decor to ensure only necessary items remain.	[ ]
Home Office: Verify that all old papers, outdated electronics, and unnecessary supplies have been cleared out.	[ ]
Storage Spaces: Check that storage areas (e.g., garage, attic) are organized and free of clutter.	[ ]
Entryway: Make sure that shoes, coats, and bags are organized and that any excess has been removed.	[ ]
Kids' Areas: Revisit toys, games, and clothing to ensure only the items in use are kept.	[ ]
Digital Spaces: Review digital files, emails, and apps to ensure they are organized and decluttered.	[ ]

Final Checklist Items	Check
Are there any remaining items that you've overlooked?	[ ]
Is there anything that doesn't belong in its current space?	[ ]
Do all your "Keep" items serve a clear purpose or bring you joy?	[ ]
Have you taken out all the trash and recycling from your decluttering sessions?	[ ]
Have you set aside items for donation or sale, and planned their next steps?	[ ]
Is your home organized in a way that makes it easy to maintain a clutter-free environment?	[ ]

Reflection Prompts	Check
How does your home feel now compared to when you started?	[ ]
What areas of your home have improved the most?	[ ]
What challenges did you overcome during your decluttering journey?	[ ]
How has decluttering impacted your mental clarity and well-being?	[ ]
What items were the hardest to let go of, and how do you feel about those decisions now?	[ ]
What would you do differently if you were to start the process over again?	[ ]

The Benefits of Eco-Friendly Decluttering

Environmental Impact

The positive impact of practicing environmentally friendly decluttering is that it helps to minimize the disposal of wastes in landfills. Reducing, reusing, rescuing, or donating are a few effective methods to reduce their ecological impacts, making living sustainably. Eco-friendly decluttering means that, when you sort through your belongings, you're not simply cleaning the house: you are helping to save the world. **Hint:** Just imagine how many fewer bags of trash you would make if you repurpose something instead of tossing it. **Guidance:** Think about the consequences of your decisions regarding decluttering for the environment in the long term. That is why, opting for sustainable solutions, you can positively influence the state of the future generations' environment. **Encouragement:** It can also be understood that any effort, no matter how minor it is, has the potential to be effective. What you get in sustainable decluttering is not only that you make a positive contribution towards the environment and the Earth's resources but also that your house gets repaired.

Mental and Emotional Benefits

Decluttering can be liberating because it also frees the mind and the spirit from what has been considered clutter. Clutter is detrimental; having a clean space means you do not have to think about irrelevant objects and other stuff around you, and life begins to take on new meaning. When you decide to choose joy and uncomplicated things, you contribute to having a joyful and more serene human existence. **Prompt:** If an item does not spark joy, a person should ask herself or himself, "How does it make me feel?" **Guidance:** Emphasize on the quality of a well-organized surrounding, the ability to concentrate, and the reduction of stress. Disorganization cannot be seen only from the aspect of space concerning objects: it is equivalent to mental disorganization.

Encouragement: Be extra pleased with the absence of clutter or clutter in your life. In doing all this, you create space for the positive things in your life and create a happier and content life.

Physical Health

The idea for a clutter-free home is that it is not only more pleasing to the eye but also beneficial for health. This way of working also entails that the living area is less cluttered and therefore the cleaning can be done effectively and will be more thorough. When you have fewer things to display, then you are reducing dust which is an important cause of allergens that circulate in the house thus improving the quality of air and health. Orderliness also has benefits for the health of an individual because it helps to reduce stress and bring order and serenity. **Hint:** Think about how much simpler it is to tidy a room if there's little debris present that is not needed. **Guidance:** Stress on the aspects of professional cleaning being valid since it promotes physical health with a clean environment. In other words, cleaning isn't about tidiness – it is about health. **Encouragement:** With each clearing activity, you not only make your house more beautiful but also less toxic and more comfortable to live in. And, your body as well as your mind will be thankful to you for this.

Community and Relationships

Decluttering is a task the object of which can bring people together, as well as make them considerably connected. The act of tidying up involves making collective donations or organizing swaps and, as such, can therefore be unifying. Dealing with donations to others is in the best interest of those in need, and comes with the additional advantages of supporting the principles of sustainability and the anti-consumerism outlook within the community. **Prompt:** Discuss the idea of the community swap – the question as used here is "What can I bring for someone else would need?" **Guidance:** Relating with people should be done while decluttering. That is why when you share the fact that you have decluttered your living space, you are making the world a better place for everybody. **Encouragement:** This way you are not only contributing to the culture that embraces sustainability and simplicity of the products but also to the culture of people who are important in our lives.

Long-Term Eco-Friendly Decluttering Habits

Consistent Decluttering

Cleaning up the place is important in ensuring that it does not accumulate clutter that will make it difficult to find items and keep the place presentable. It's better to determine periods when it is necessary to sort things, 3 months may be enough; one can also use vernal, summer, autumn, and winter as indicators of when it is time to sort things. Forcing, and establishing routines that would allow constant maintenance of the decluttering activities provides the best way of maintaining the order without the need to declutter again in the future. **Hint:** Schedule a bi-weekly blitz day so that it's not such a daunting task to tackle—instead, it is something that you do regularly. **Guidance:** Consistency is key. It is therefore important, to declutter as often as possible, to avoid being bogged down by clutter. **Encouragement:** This way, the process of decluttering turns into a habit and the living space is being tidied up and invigorated over and over. It is just a little you can do for your house and for your mind to be at ease.

Mindful Consumption

Eco-friendly decluttering should also be translated into reasonable and conscious consumption of products. Plan your purchases, do not buy things that do not bring value to the life you are living. Take measures that can help one not to give in to the temptations of shopping and shop sustainably, that is select greener products and patronize organizations that uphold sustainability. **Prompt:** Some practical questions to ask before making a purchase are 'Do I need this?', 'how will this affect the space?' **Guidance:** Be conscious of one's consumption habits. This way, you get more intentional with the belongings you allow to enter your home, there is less demand for constant cleaning and decluttering, and everyone wins. **Encouragement:** Every decision made consciously helps to create a tidy and beautiful home, as well as a home in which the owner cares for the planet and tries to reduce waste.

Creative Reuse and Upcycling

Creative recycling or cycling as they are often called are fantastic ways of continuing the method of decluttering while saving the environment from further pollution. Go on viewing objects with different uses or converting objects into functions or ornaments in your house. Participate in projects that are oriented for the general benefit of society and pass on your skills and knowledge of upcycling and recycling. **Hint:** Novelty application—imagine, little as it seems at first glance, what you can build using elements that you are nevertheless going to throw away. **Guidance:** Be as resourceful as possible, to get more useful time out of items. To me upcycling not only is cheaper and friendlier to the environment, but also makes the interior closer to you. **Encouragement:** If you take a Creative reuse approach then you are converting- clutter to opportunity, revamping your place full of creativity and concern. It is a satisfying way to help maintain many environments and at the same time bring more personality into many homes.

Embracing the Minimalist Mindset

Learn to free yourself and be happy with as little as possible. When you remove the superfluous; the desire for material things, and meaningless attitudes and activities, you can create a healthier and more purposeful life. This is not to mention the customer's benefit of having a mind that is free of clutter due to this minimalist perspective. **Prompt:** Consider what makes you happy—can you downgrade and be happier? **Guidance:** That's because many people become focused on the tangible assets and the physical manifestations of success rather than actual joy and happiness. It's not a way of thinking about life as a kind of scarcity mentality, a lack mentality, or what I call a 'less is less' mentality. **Encouragement:** Simplicity can make life more rich and fulfilling, having the least hindrances having the most effect can be interesting. In purging yourself, you create space for the essential things in life, thereby, increasing your level of fulfillment.

Day 29:
Celebrate Your Wins and Create a Maintenance Plan

Celebrating Your Wins	**Check**
Take a moment to enjoy the simplicity and organization you've created.	[ ]
Share your success with friends or on social media to inspire others.	[ ]
Treat yourself to a small reward for completing the decluttering journey.	[ ]
Reflect on the positive changes in your environment and mindset.	[ ]
Write about your experience and how it has impacted your life.	[ ]
Host a gathering in your newly organized space to celebrate with loved ones.	[ ]
Creating a Maintenance Plan	**Check**
Set up a regular schedule for decluttering sessions (e.g., monthly, seasonally).	[ ]
Implement the "One In, One Out" rule to prevent future clutter accumulation.	[ ]
Establish designated spaces for items to keep your home organized.	[ ]
Create a list of daily, weekly, and monthly tasks to maintain cleanliness and organization.	[ ]
Consider using a decluttering app or planner to track your progress and stay motivated.	[ ]
Regularly review and update your goals to align with your evolving lifestyle.	[ ]
Final Reflection Prompts	**Check**
How do you plan to maintain the simplicity and organization you've achieved?	[ ]
What strategies will you use to prevent clutter from returning?	[ ]
How has your perspective on material possessions changed?	[ ]
What has been the most rewarding part of your decluttering journey?	[ ]
How will you continue to simplify and improve your life moving forward?	[ ]
Action	**Check**
Celebrate the completion of your decluttering journey with a meaningful activity.	[ ]
Share your decluttering success and tips with others to inspire their journeys.	[ ]
Create a maintenance plan that works for your lifestyle to keep your space clutter-free.	[ ]
Reflect on your journey and set new goals for maintaining a minimalist, joyful life.	[ ]

Conclusion

Recap of Eco-Friendly Decluttering: There are so many reasons why using the eco-friendly approach to the removal of unwanted items has its advantages; some of which include; When practices are put into place and spaces are decluttered you simultaneously declutter the landfills and promote the use of eco-friendly products that benefit you and your neighbors.

Embracing the Journey: Find fun and ways in which you can make the journey of going green in the process of decluttering fun. You must remember that this is not some obsessive-compulsive disorder about cleaning, it is about making the right choices. A good attitude to the process is to always feel happy while making the necessary changes for a better life.

Looking Forward: In the long run, it becomes easy to see that the payoff of having a clutter-free, sustainable life is possible. But if you are determined to turn a new page and daily get into the habit of managing and consuming, then you are on the path to a future that is full of hope, peace, and meaning. Freedom and the appreciation of the positive contribution towards your own life and the world is gained from less.

Chapter 9: Time Management for Decluttering: Efficient Schedules and Routines (Because Procrastination is a Real Thing)

Setting Realistic Goals: Rome Wasn't Decluttered in a Day

Importance of Small, Achievable Goals

As for the process of de-cluttering, having a small and gradual approach is the best course of action. To make the task more manageable, decide on one drawer, shelf, or corner then try to organize all the room at once. With each advancement, every win – no matter how insignificant it may be – builds towards others and ensures that you get further, and further while providing the morale boost needed to keep striving. This means it is better to approach the task systematically – a little clean-up now and then is better than being stressed out, you have a monumental cleaning session once a week. This way, you avoid quick burnout and you constantly work on eliminating the mess without getting too frustrated. **Hint:** Divide work into sections that are easy to accomplish and award yourself for each completed fragment. **Guidance:** First, focus on the less cluttered spaces to create the steam, and remember that any organizing process is not a race. **Encouragement:** I'm quite convinced now that the wheel turns from small steps, however, revolutionary quite often is the result. When you mark attainable goals, you ensure that you get to win and build good habits for keeping your space clean.

Effective Time Management

Time management is very important especially when you are planning to declutter your space. Choose specific hours in a week and try to clean only during those hours and nothing else. And the beauty of it is, you get to declutter incrementally because you're doing it as part of a schedule, so progress is ongoing. To make the process more fun and less oppressive, try such things as setting alarms and giving oneself treats after completion of a particular session. Proactively sort out the chores by targeting the greatest niches that, when cleared, will create immense impact. **Prompt:** Ask yourself, "Which areas will give the most gratification when sorted?" **Rule of thumb:** Be realistic to avoid burnout. Just as it's better to write for a certain number of hours daily than to cram the whole day in one day and completely drain yourself out. **Encouragement:** Scheduling time for cleaning up not only results in a clean environment but also clears the mind thus enabling one to live life to the fullest.

Family Involvement

Decluttering may be done as a task involving different members of the same family. Improve the level of engagement in children by making tidying up an activity that is a complete joy for children and even adults. This could be in the form of a game or a challenge that involves the children to avoid the monotonous look of the whole process. Divide work so that all members of the family are given particular roles that they are to undertake. **Hint:** One way to do this is with a chore chart so that a household is a team and everyone must pitch in to declutter. **Guidance:** Promote incentives for the work done by all, e.g. when the house is decluttered everyone gets to watch a movie or has a treat. **Encouragement:** But it's the celebration of the journey that should be done side by side. As a family, decluttering helps family members relieve the burden and, at the same time, become closer and learn important lessons concerning cleanliness and order. **Prompt:** Sit with your family members and ask them — for example, Where can we tidy up and make the living process less interlinked for all of us?

Emotional Aspects of Decluttering

Decluttering is not only about cleaning simply; it is about purging, and that is a spiritual process. Concede that decluttering can be quite difficult, particularly if one is parting with belongings with particular attachment values. This helps because it begins with tackling less charged-up items which in turn helps develop confidence in handling the rest of the items. It is less confrontational because gradual progress enables you to go through your attachments at your own pace. **Guidance:** Tackle every item with the attitude of opening new possibilities in one's life instead of seeing what is being taken away. **Encouragement:** Freedom of emotion is a liberty that can be enjoyed after ridding oneself of unnecessary materialistic things. If you always remember your past you will never have a future you are preparing for. **Prompt:** Use the main idea of how one has to free up space to unlock opportunities which hold the key to happiness.

Maintenance Checklist

Purpose: To ensure that your space remains clutter-free after the initial decluttering, this checklist helps you stay on track with regular maintenance tasks.

Weekly Maintenance Checklist

Task	Check
Tidy up the entryway (shoes, coats, bags)	[ ]
Clear kitchen counters of clutter and unused items	[ ]
Sort and recycle junk mail	[ ]
Wipe down surfaces in living areas	[ ]
Organize and return misplaced items to their designated spots	[ ]
Do a quick sweep of high-traffic areas for stray items	[ ]
Check fridge for leftovers and expired food	[ ]
Empty trash bins and recycling	[ ]

Monthly Maintenance Checklist

Task	Check
Deep clean the kitchen (including fridge and pantry)	[ ]
Review and declutter closet (remove unworn items)	[ ]
Organize bathroom cabinets (check for expired products)	[ ]
Dust and declutter shelves, bookcases, and decor	[ ]
Review and organize paper files in the home office	[ ]
Vacuum and clean under furniture	[ ]
Wash and rotate bedding and seasonal items	[ ]
Donate or discard items you haven't used in the past month	[ ]

Maintenance Checklist

Seasonal Maintenance Checklist

Season	Task	Check
Spring	Rotate seasonal clothing	[ ]
	Declutter and clean outdoor areas	[ ]
	Check and declutter storage spaces (e.g., garage)	[ ]
Summer	Organize outdoor equipment and tools	[ ]
	Deep clean windows and window treatments	[ ]
	Review and declutter kids' toys and summer gear	[ ]
Fall	Organize seasonal decor and holiday items	[ ]
	Prepare and declutter for back-to-school	[ ]
	Clean and organized kitchen for holiday cooking	[ ]
Winter	Declutter and organize holiday decor storage	[ ]
	Check for worn-out winter clothing and accessories	[ ]
	Plan for the New Year: declutter and set new goals	[ ]

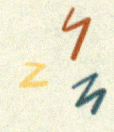

Creating a Decluttering Schedule: Making Time for Tidiness

Assessing the Chaos

Before one can begin the procedure of decluttering, he or she needs to take a look at the mess. Record the various rooms or other areas that are likely to attract attention, especially those with much litter or high traffic. To get the most out of the efforts it is advised to prioritize the following rooms. In this case, be sure to set flexible time targets for each of the goals you set to make them achievable. **Hint:** First of all, target high-profile areas — where the information, when arranged properly, will be especially helpful. **Guidance:** This means that if a project has many activities, they should be subdivided to make the load to be handled more manageable. **Encouragement:** Just know the fact that evaluation of the mess is the primary step toward engineering the mess into order. **Prompt:** Thus, you should always be guided by the question "Which of the areas will make me the most content once it is clean?"

Short, Focused Sessions

Since decluttering does not have to be done in one go, short focused sessions are more efficient in terms of energy. Tell yourself strictly to set a particular time for example 20-30 minutes and be devoted to that particular time only. This approach reduces exhaustion and thus enhances morale when carrying out the plans thus enhancing efficiency. The use of the to-do list is that you can track your progress, so, having completed tasks, you will be able to see that you have achieved something. **Hint:** Take time to appreciate the smaller successes, for instance, by cleaning a drawer or arranging the items on a shelf, and then you get goodies afterward. **Guidance:** This is better for productivity—short bright sessions can be done every day or near each other and the total amount of work completed will be impressive. **Encouragement:** This way the activity is not overwhelming and it is easier to complete the decluttering process because a little goes a long way. **Prompt:** Think how great it is to watch even a small area that has been changed by your actions.

Family Decluttering Days

Decluttering should become a fun family activity and this can be done by setting proper family decluttering days. Enable children to have fun to make them work hard and do what they would not like to do as what they are being made to do is a game. Paint the process fun – As much as possible integrate music into the process and small rewards in equal measures. **Hint:** Make it a memory-making event by taking 'before' and 'after' pictures of quests you both complete together. **Guidance:** Every individual in the family should be given particular duties to make them understand that the work should be done as a team. **Encouragement:** Aside from making your home neater, organizing your family's clutter would also make for great fun and is a surefire way of making your family come closer as one. **Prompt:** Before sitting down together, turn to your fellow family members and request them to say, "What in our family can we do today to make it more comfortable for all of us?"

Digital Decluttering

Just as with the physical clutter, the digital one should not be neglected, it is a severe nuisance that will affect your workflow. Have weekly digital tidy sessions to help in the organization of the devices you use. The file is to concentrate on how to arrange files and put them in order depending on the time, subject, or any way that would facilitate their search. In your email, it is advisable to manage it and delete the unnecessary messages it collects to avoid cramming. **Hint:** Utilize technology when it comes to other functions which can be partly done by the technology, for instance, the use of mail and photos. **Guidance:** Integrate digital decluttering into people's daily existence by scheduling it together with physical decluttering during the change of each season.

Encouragement: To take the stigma away from the phrase; deleting items from your lawn, cleaning your room, or decluttering your home is always easier and much more productive than having a cluttered space around you – the same goes for our digital lives. **Prompt:** Think of the benefits of having a clean virtual space to the efficiency and the general well-being of an individual.

Strategies for Efficient Decluttering

Focus on High-Impact Areas

While choosing the areas to declutter, it is crucial to limit yourself to the most used zones in your home at first. The area of starting is the kitchen and the living room because people tend to spend a lot of time there. A clean and uncluttered kitchen is good for preparing food and easy to work in while a clean living room invites neighbors to sit and relax. After the living room, focus on redecorating the bedroom and making it as comfortable as possible to be able to get a good night's sleep. Do not neglect your bathroom; the organization of this area guarantees a good start in the morning. Finally, organize a clean hall that reflects the welcoming character you want to set when you and any guest welcome himself or herself in the house. **Hint:** In one place begin and follow it through gradually. **Guidance:** Giving focus on these areas can greatly enhance the usage and ambiance of your house. **Encouragement:** This way, you will start feeling a difference almost immediately in other aspects of your life that these spaces affect.

Decluttering Tools and Supplies

Ensuring that one has the right equipment and items to use in the process of decluttering can help in making the exercise easier and not tiresome. The first step is to ensure that there are containers such as boxes bags, labels, and cleaning materials needed to sort out the items. Organize your things properly using organizational tools like storage bins, baskets as well as dividers. **Hint:** Always have a donation center available for use, so when you can donate, it becomes easy in the process of getting rid of the clutter that is in your home. **Guidance:** Provide yourself with a system to sort your loads of trash so that, when you are decluttering your home, you do so in an environmentally friendly manner. **Encouragement:** Not having to go back and forth to read the docs, having everything in one place makes the process easier and keeps things moving. **Prompt:** Check, "Do I have all the things that I need to be successful?" This way you minimize distractions and focus on the necessary work at hand.

Motivation and Rewards

There is always a common tendency to get bored halfway through the process of decluttering, it is important to remain focused to the end. It is also important that before you begin the process of a particular session, you have a set objective of what exactly should be achieved for the period, for instance arranging a particular room or a segment of the house. **Hint:** Subdivide activities or projects that are seen to take a long time so that they do not elicit feelings of overburdening. **Guidance:** Hitting a few benchmarks entitles you to some good things usually including snacks, break time, and any other thing that calms you down. It can also be advisable to visualize success as an excellent motivator to help bring about success. Having a 'wish list' or 'progress log' where you can paste pictures or write about the gains you envision enjoying may motivate you. **Encouragement:** Having a workout buddy means you are committed to exercising with someone you know and this acts as a motivator. **Prompt:** Asking yourself, 'What can I give myself for doing this again tomorrow?' will transform the chore of decluttering into an exciting and fulfilling task.

Maintaining Decluttering Momentum

If you have removed clutter from your house, then certain precautionary measures should be taken to ensure that they do not infiltrate your house again. Conduct surveys occasionally to ascertain its performance and review the plan and strategy when it is necessary. **Hint:** Be ready to change, this is an essential concept of your life; you cannot stick to one program and one diet for the rest of your life. **Guidance:** Adopt practices that prevent clutter from recurring; where applicable, ensure that the items are rearranged at the close of the day. **Encouragement:** Do not forget to mark the different stages of the decluttering process with a little party cheer or celebration. Therefore the outcomes appear plausible and maintain enjoyment for those participating to ensure the right behaviors are encouraged. **Prompt:** Another question could be, "What am I proud of myself for today?" These questions keep you on track, not to overlook the small victories one gains most of the time.

Sentimental Items Reflection Chart

Purpose: To help you thoughtfully consider which sentimental items to keep and which to let go, this chart guides your reflection process.

Sentimental Items Reflection Prompts

Item	Why Am I Keeping This?	Is It Time to Let Go?	Action	Check
Example: Old Love Letters	They remind me of a past relationship but bring up more sadness than joy	Yes, they no longer serve a positive purpose	Take a photo, then let them go	[ ]
Childhood Toys	They represent happy memories, but I have outgrown them	Yes, these memories can be cherished without the toys	Donate to a children's charity	[ ]
Family Heirlooms	They hold family history but don't fit into my current lifestyle	No, but I will store them safely	Preserve and store properly	[ ]
Travel Souvenirs	They remind me of trips but are gathering dust	Yes, I can keep photos or a journal instead	Create a travel photo album	[ ]
Photos of Past Events	They capture important moments but many are duplicates or blurry	Yes, keep only the best	Organize and digitize photos	[ ]

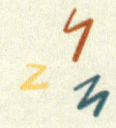

Sentimental Items Reflection Chart

Reflection Questions

Question	Check
Does this item bring more joy or more burden to my life?	[ ]
Am I holding onto this item out of guilt or obligation?	[ ]
Would I keep this item if I were starting fresh today?	[ ]
How can I honor the memory without keeping the physical item?	[ ]
Would this item be more meaningful to someone else?	[ ]

Actions Based on Reflection

Action	Check
Take photos of items before letting them go	[ ]
Write a journal entry about the memories attached to an item	[ ]
Store only the most meaningful items in a dedicated memory box	[ ]
Donate or give away items to those who will appreciate them	[ ]
Release items that no longer serve a positive purpose	[ ]

Long-Term Decluttering Success

Sustainable Habits

A timely routine is essential for the maintenance and long-term accomplishment of decluttering. One possible manner of preventing clutter accumulation is to establish habitual daily chores; for instance, making sure the room is cleaned before going to bed. **Hint:** Weekly cleaning sessions mean that you do not have to undertake major makeovers for the house to be orderly. **Guidance:** It is recommended that you should do a monthly check-up of your space to make the necessary changes so that it is in harmony with your lifestyle. Keep daily cleaning to a minimum during the day, and make a schedule for deep cleanings of certain areas during the time of the year when the mess is most likely to accumulate. **Encouragement:** The idea is to establish routines that will keep the house clean but with little bursts of labor that require lots of effort. **Prompt:** The approach one should take is asking the question, "What small habit can I start today?" You are more likely to stick to a plan of creating new habits that will enable you to cease cluttering your life.

Mindful Consumption

Being mindful of what you purchase and owning only what you truly need can go a long way in warding off clutter. Intentionally buy things—do not buy unthinkingly, but rather, think about whether you require a certain product. They include; focusing on the quality of things you buy rather than the quantity, only buying good things which may be needed or will give you a lot of joy. **Hint:** One way of trying to manage how to reduce cluttering is that you have to minimize the number of items you bring into your home. **Guidance:** People should be persuaded to give experiences instead of things this encourages the reduction of clutter and also parties to the creation of fond memories. **Encouragement:** By implementing these practices, you are not only reducing the complexity of your existence but applying a more conscious approach to consumption. **Prompt:** You should never buy something and wonder, 'Did this enhance my home or my life?' Choosing to make better decisions for the appearance of your home can make such a difference.

Minimalist Mindset

One of the key areas that need to be fostered to avoid cluttering is the ability to adopt a minimalist approach to life. Opt for simplicity as a way of appreciating what is of value to you in life. Focus on the quality of relations or the experiences rather than the acquisition of things which usually makes us happier. **Hint:** Often practicing the feeling of thankfulness for what one has can go a long way in changing the attitude from seeking more to being content with what one possesses. **Guidance:** Reduce is always good; always try to reduce and make your space look good to make an informed decision that has to do with changing your environment. **Encouragement:** Minimalism is not about sacrifice; far from it, it is a way to enrich one's life and simplify it by shedding all pointless weight. **Prompt:** The very question proposed here is, "How can I unclutter today?" such a question is not Specific but it keeps on applying the process, thus ensuring a clutter-free and fulfilling life.

Reflect and Adjust

Reflection follows as it is a vital tool used in the decluttering process. Make it a culture to set aside time to think through the experience and how you feel the change has affected you. But in most cases, the goals should be fluid and change with time depending on the results of the assessments made in line with the specified needs of the persons involved. **Hint:** Recognising your advances, however minor, maintains your morale and reminds you of the changes you are implementing. **Guidance:** Stay motivated by continuously learning about minimalism and the process of letting go. Engage with books, blogs, friends, and others in the course to support your journey. **Encouragement:** When you reflect, you gain awareness regarding the advantages that can be culled from de-cluttering and the reasons why one should not default back to messy habits. **Prompt:** One should come up with a question like; 'what have I realized from decluttering so far?' This leads to an increased understanding of the whole process and keeps one motivated in the pursuit of the goal in the long run.

Conclusion

Recap of Time Management Strategies: Essentials of decluttering entail aim setting to be realistic and plan towards a successful decluttering campaign. To this end, by dis-suspending work activities into more manageable chunks and concentrating on key priorities, one can go a long way and not necessarily get bogged down in the process. Cues can be arranged to reconfirm to you on the appropriateness or need to change the process of decluttering hence making it sustainable in the future.

Encouragement for Consistency: The way of life to keep the environment free from clutter should be adopted regularly. Small steps of cleanliness can go a long way to avert a relapse, to a state of clutter in the home. It emphasizes that you must include rigid schedules and plans as well as keep the free spirit of the company in mind and never forget adaptability as one of your key tools. Bear in mind that decluttering is a process that is not limited to several hours, days, or weeks but is a lifelong process, and by being constant you will manage to remain on the right path.

Looking Forward: The significance of keeping a neat and clean home cannot be underestimated for it has lifelong gains as we have seen. But, there are also other defined benefits that you already mentioned – you will feel more orderly and liberated, stress-free, and with a clear mind, while your home will be organized and aligned with your priorities. With each small advancement, one sets the foundation for happiness, imagination, and a new improved existence to continue the journey to a deliberate and purposeful life.

Final Motivational Note: So to declutter and tidy up, take the approach with a spirit of fun and extra effort. Avoid getting lost in the process and remind yourself of the goal each day: a home, a life liberated from the tyranny of too much stuff. Don't lose heart, don't lose passion, and always bear in mind that the move you are making will take you closer to where you want to be. You've got this!

Chapter 10: Decluttering for Seniors: Tailored Approaches for Aging Adults (With a Side of Humor)

Understanding Unique Challenges: It's Not Just About the Stuff

The Emotional Baggage of Belongings

Decluttering is not only a process related to objects; it is a psychologist's voyage through memories and feelings. Every single object may have some kind of burden of the past behind it and the whole procedure appears to be rather existential. Personal belongings can also be a problem to be parted with mainly because allegiance may be made on sentimental items such as mementos that depict special moments or people. But that is a foreign past and it is important to know that these possessions are not you – they are memories of a past self, not the self you are now. **Hint:** You might want to ask yourself 'Does this have a place of joy in my life today or is it a placeholder merely for what once was'. These questions will assist in deciding what stays. **Guidance:** It is acceptable to keep a few d'orianz treasures but now that we all want to declutter, learning how to let go of each other. **Encouragement:** Forgetting doesn't mean that you are discarding something; rather, it means that you are giving room to something else.

Family Clutter Dynamics

Family clutter is a process, more often than not a continuous one, of inheriting, accumulating, and neglecting belongings. Being able to understand this is a way through which people can be ready to declutter, and do it with jokes and smiling. Engaging all the family members is also helpful not only because it relieves the workload but also makes organizing a fun family activity. **Hint:** Hire your children to help you declutter, as if it is a task like spring cleaning or end-year-cleaning. **Guidance:** According to personal invention, this can be used to tell stories about items and to encourage young ones about what they wish to retain. This can help assist with the process of decluttering because allowing go of things can be so emotional. **Encouragement:** Not that one has to, but it is recommended that one should take photographs, write a diary, or scrapbook the funny and tender moments. This makes decluttering more of a process of bonding with the family while making memories in the process of elimination.

Digital Clutter Challenges

Digital clutter is not any different from physical clutter; it hides in the background of our technology. First of all, one must remember that this concept is all about a mental as well as a spatial mess. **Hint:** It might be helpful to schedule a designated 'spring clean' for your screens every month or so, where you dedicate some time to organization and mental takedown to your devices. **Guidance:** First of all, sort the documents that are kept in computers—make folders, delete twofold documents, and save significant documents. **Prompt:** This question as simple as it is effective will assist one in the process of organizing them about what to keep and what to delete. **Encouragement:** Typically, people organize their electronic documents, and as you go through these documents, you may discover items that are pleasing to the eye such as old photos. Celebrate these small discoveries as part of the decluttering journey, knowing that each step brings you closer to digital clarity and peace.

The Journey of Self-Discovery

The process of decluttering is not only about removing things from our physical environments but also it is, in essence, a transformative introspective experience. When organizing your property you may discover that it is easier to let go of the past and advance in one's state of emotional and psychological development. **Hint:** Praise yourself for each success, no matter how trivial – organizing your closet, or letting go of an object with sentimental value. There is almost a shift from one chapter in life to another in each step that is taken forward. **Guidance:** When facing difficulties that occur, try to make jokes since laughter will help to share the burden and the process will be more cheerful. **Encouragement:** Relax with the new changes that come with following a new lifestyle, one of decluttering. Remember that forgiveness is not just a process of release from the past but the process of creating space for new experiences to live a life of purpose.

Room-by-Room Declutter Guide

Purpose: This guide helps you systematically declutter each room, focusing on specific areas and items that commonly accumulate clutter.

Living Room Declutter Guide

Area	Items to Declutter	Check
Bookshelves	Books you've read and don't plan to reread	[ ]
	Magazines, newspapers, and catalogs	[ ]
	DVDs, CDs, or games you no longer use	[ ]
Coffee Table	Old remotes, coasters, or decor you no longer like	[ ]
	Unused candles or candle holders	[ ]
	Magazines, papers, and other clutter	[ ]
Entertainment Center	Outdated electronics or media devices	[ ]
	Wires, cables, and chargers are no longer in use	[ ]
Decor	Outdated or unwanted decor items	[ ]
	Frames with photos you no longer want to display	[ ]

Kitchen Declutter Guide

Area	Items to Declutter	Check
Pantry	Expired or stale food items	[ ]
	Duplicate or unused kitchen gadgets	[ ]
Drawers	Utensils you never use, broken items	[ ]
	Takeout menus, expired coupons, and junk mail	[ ]
Counters	Appliances or tools you rarely use	[ ]
	Paper piles, keys, or other non-kitchen items	[ ]
Fridge	Expired condiments, leftovers, and food past its prime	[ ]

Bedroom Declutter Guide

Area	Items to Declutter	Check
Closet	Clothes you no longer wear or that don't fit	[ ]
	Worn-out shoes and accessories	[ ]
	Old handbags or luggage	[ ]
Dresser	Old jewelry, watches, or accessories	[ ]
	Outdated or worn-out undergarments and socks	[ ]
Nightstand	Old books, magazines, and clutter	[ ]
	Chargers or electronics you no longer use	[ ]

Tips for Gentle Decluttering: Because Patience is a Virtue

Starting Small

I learned that decluttering is something that takes time, it is not a one-day mission. Education has to be seen as a chronic process and not as an action that is going to show positive outcomes shortly. Starting with the simplest projects is okay; one may start by decluttering a single drawer or closet. **Hint:** This is why a 15-minute timer should be set and work done with the focus on one area at a time. This helps in avoiding cases of getting overwhelmed and as such makes the task seem much simpler. **Guidance:** Take a break and congratulate yourself when you complete a drawer or clear a countertop. Success paves the way for an approach to other gigantic tasks. **Encouragement:** As I mentioned, small progress is also progress, since, in our line of work, we never encounter big changes. Every single action taken on the way leads you to the ultimate aim of a clutter-free and serene environment and hence the process is very rewarding.

Engaging Family Members

The provision of decluttering does not necessarily have to be individualistic – turn the process into a game and include the family. Perhaps you can transform it into an activity in which everyone will engage, for example, through creating tasks or incentives for participation. **Hint:** Organise a point system that would see children get specific points for certain items that they help in removing. This point can be cashed in for some prizes such as candies or even additional time for play. **Guidance:** This is an excellent chance to explain to younger members of the family the importance of simple and well-organized living. It is a nice method of transitioning essential life skills to the next generation. **Encouragement:** Some of the skills taught while cleaning are, instead of just tidying, you are making memories with the family as well as strengthening the relationship. This process can be almost as much about relations as it can be related to cleanliness, which adds more sense to the process for all the people involved.

Digital Decluttering Strategies

Like physical clutter, there needs to be a periodic cleaning out of digital clutter as well. Just like with physical clutter, the more time passes, the worse it gets, so make it a point to have weekly or monthly 'cleans' for your digital abode. **Hint:** One should begin by the process of opting out of the various lists that the person rarely reads and are just taking up space in the list of received emails. **Guidance:** Get the files and other documents electronic to facilitate easy storage and to ensure that they are easily accessed by everyone. **Prompt:** You should ask yourself 'Does this add value to my digital life, or just a noise?'; This kind of practice can assist one in minimizing unnecessary items. **Encouragement:** Digital decluttering can be a lifelong practice, and each session, although not entirely painless, does feel much more in line with my 'ideal'. That way, you save time on digital noise and make room for interaction and material that benefits you in the real world.

Emotional Self-Care

Before you start the process of decluttering, make sure that you treat yourself with kindness all through the process. Since this can be a process emotionally taxing it's important to be kind to ourselves. **Hint:** Have a Memory Box for special items—this way there is no need to retain so many items in the house even if their sentimental value cannot be overemphasized. **Guidance:** Decluttering is a process of becoming and is not about getting it right. Do not despair if as you go through the steps, you take your time or even have to take a break to think. **Encouragement:** Practise mindfulness to remain focused and mentally present during the process of decluttering. Whenever the anxiety- or doubt-creatures come creeping around, pause for a moment take a deep breath, and tell yourself that you are making the space better and more mindful. This process is not merely about arranging the metric of our lives, but about reorganizing the heart and every small accomplishment is a triumph.

Strategies for Embracing Minimalism: The Joy of Saying No to Stuff

Handling Free Stuff

Everyone loves free items but before you grab that free pen or mug, it is necessary to consider if it needs to make the trip back to your house. One has to wonder whether a presented item will really be of any use or whether it will just accumulate dust. **Hint:** With a freebie in hand, the receiver may perhaps think that much pleasure can be derived or much need the item may meet. If it's just going to sit in a corner, unopened and unused, it may be better to decline. To be minimalistic, one has to understand that they have to sometimes decline free items that will clutter up space in their home. To any of these freebies that have actual value, consider how you might recycle them or give them a new use. **Guidance:** Reuse a free tote bag as a shopper bag instead of using disposable shopping bags. **Encouragement:** What is more impressive here is the fact that, while turning down all the freebies with such wording, one not only avoids adding more clutter to the place but also gets a chance to enjoy a clear mind.

Dealing with Emotional Clutter

Chasing emotions is many times difficult, but that is where the "Maybe Later" box comes in handy. This shifting solution enables you to put aside anything you feel you want to 'part with' but do not want to throw away just yet. **Prompt:**

When it comes to your possessions, question if an item still makes you as happy as it used to, if not, put it in the box and review it at a later date. **Guidance:** The items that were created this year should probably be revisited in a few months; set a reminder in your calendar. This will give you more time for emotions to die down and hence come up with an effective decision. **Encouragement:** Decluttering of emotional baggage is a process. Relish every milestone that you make as you admire the works you have been able to produce.

Family Decluttering Strategies

The process of decluttering can be entertaining and even turn into a great family activity. Make it a treasure hunt where your children will be required to look or search for things that they do not need around the house. **Hint:** Give them incentives such as stickers or more play times for everything they decide to leave behind. This makes the process interesting and hence individuals are encouraged to be part of the process. **Guidance:** Attitude to conform the decluttering as a way of imparting skills of organization and the essence of keeping only items that bring joy or are essential. **Encouragement:** Take photos before, and after the process and mark special occasions together in the process of decluttering with your family. These collective tasks are beneficial not only for cleaning the house but also for forming nice associations with the process of tidying up, and, of course, for the unity of family members. Strengthening decluttering is a special task that is completed by all members of the family, you maintain the clean space and also teach the members of the household to think about tidiness and cleanliness as the common goal.

Digital Decluttering Strategies

Clutter in the digital world can be equally disturbing as clutter in the physical world. Implement a weekly practice of a no-technology day, where the accounts have to be 'Unplugged and Purged'. Prompt: For example, before downloading a new application ask yourself, "Do I need this app?". If you don't need it, it's high time to delete it. It is unwise to have files scattered around with no particular pattern; one should create folders and then categories of the files that ease the search process. **Hint:** A lot of them, just like pop-up ads are distractions that should be switched off so that you can attend to what is important. **Guidance:** Bits of information that have not been accessed for a long time should be deleted, as well as files, e-mails as well as applications that have been uninstalled for a long time. **Encouragement:** it clears your digital life, and makes your experiences intentional instead of aimless thus making digital life less stressful and more productive. The act of decluttering the messages, emails, apps, and digital documents, gives you back the reins of your gadgets and helps you get your head in a better state for more fulfilling endeavors.

Digital Declutter Checklist

Purpose: To help you organize and streamline your digital life, this checklist guides you through decluttering your digital spaces, including files, emails, apps, and more.

Email Declutter Checklist

Task	Check
Unsubscribe from newsletters and mailing lists you no longer read	[ ]
Delete old emails that are no longer relevant	[ ]
Organize important emails into folders or labels	[ ]
Set up filters to automatically sort incoming emails	[ ]
Empty your spam and junk mail folders	[ ]
Archive emails that you need to keep but don't need immediate access to	[ ]
Delete or archive old sent emails	[ ]

File and Document Declutter Checklist

Task	Check
Delete duplicate or outdated files	[ ]
Organize files into clearly labeled folders	[ ]
Back up important documents to an external hard drive or cloud storage	[ ]
Delete downloaded files that are no longer needed	[ ]
Empty the recycle bin or trash folder on your computer	[ ]
Organize photos into albums and delete duplicates	[ ]
Remove old or unused software programs	[ ]

Digital Declutter Checklist

Device Declutter Checklist

Task	Check
Delete apps you no longer use on your phone, tablet, or computer	[ ]
Organize apps into folders for easy access	[ ]
Clear cache and unnecessary data to free up space	[ ]
Update software and apps to the latest versions	[ ]
Back up important data from devices	[ ]
Delete old text messages or conversations that are no longer relevant	[ ]
Organize your phone's home screen for efficiency	[ ]

Social Media Declutter Checklist

Task	Check
Unfollow accounts that no longer inspire or add value to your life	[ ]
Clean up your friends or follower list	[ ]
Delete old posts or photos that no longer reflect who you are	[ ]
Organize your social media feeds to prioritize content that matters	[ ]
Turn off notifications for non-essential apps	[ ]
Review and adjust your privacy settings	[ ]
Take a digital detox by scheduling regular breaks from social media	[ ]

Final Digital Declutter Actions

Action	Check
Set up a regular schedule for digital decluttering (e.g., monthly, quarterly)	[ ]
Create a digital filing system that's easy to maintain	[ ]
Ensure all important data is backed up regularly	[ ]
Simplify your digital life by using only the apps and tools that serve you best	[ ]
Reflect on how digital decluttering has improved your focus and well-being	[ ]

The Benefits of Minimalist Living for Seniors

Mental Clarity

Clutter can greatly hinder the ability of elderly people to achieve mental calm, and it is therefore important to ensure that a home is free from clutter. Getting rid of clutter helps to ease pressure or tension and therefore enables one to be relaxed hence improving productivity. **Hint:** Squaring away your things can assist in relieving your thoughts and focus on responsibilities or even on the beauty of your environment. **Guidance:** Concentrate on having only objects that one has a positive feeling about or objects that are useful in some way. **Encouragement:** Decluttering means that as you are removing items from your home, the happiness that rises from clearing your space is multiplied by the number of items that you are removing. Less complicated living not only allows for easier navigation of day-to-day interactions but also allows space that can be enjoyed as a result of its organization. As people grow older, they should try and live a simple life, one that is less troubled by issues to do with property and the like.

Physical Health

Getting rid of those unnecessary things can have various beneficial impacts on your physical health as well. A neat and well-arranged environment makes it convenient to manage social order, resulting in sound health. **Hint:** Think about how much less likely you are to trip or have an accident given that there will be less to trip over. **Guidance:** Prefer organizing the space from which the density of furniture and other items hampers the inhabitants' free movement and circulation. **Encouragement:** Every item that is taken out of the dwelling brings one closer to a healthier and safer environment. In this way, the desire to keep a clean and tidy home helps one build an environment that will directly have an impact on one's physical well-being and therefore enable him or her to perform day-to-day activities independently. By practicing minimalism, you know that your home is secure and that you have freedom of movement, an absence of clutter, and safety, all the things that will help you have a clear mind.

Improved Relationships

Clutter in a home affects one's self and interpersonal relationships negatively; therefore, living in a clean space is advantageous. Eradicating clutter decreases tension because conflicts and the resulting unpleasantness are drowned in cleanliness, and family members are happier. **Hint:** These are some of the advantages of organizing your time; you'll spend less time picking items off of the floor, thus spending more time with family. **Guidance:** During the decluttering process you can take the opportunity to engage in fun activities that shall have bonded the family. **Encouragement:** When doing the cleaning, it is done together hence improving the communication and cooperation among the family members. Thus, practicing does make a way, when you make an environment that is coherent for living and fosters proper relationships among the family members. Clutter is no longer an individual problem but a responsibility to be addressed together, it connects you with your family and makes the home environment happy and collaborative.

Embracing Change

The concept of minimalism is simple and means living a life that is free from a lot of things. Essentially, by shifting your perspective to what matters most, that is, experiencing, relationship, and personal development, one is likely to transition to other life stages easily. **Prompt:** As you tour through your new phase of life, ask yourself, "What gives me the most joy?" This should guide you on what to hold onto and what to discard. **Guidance:** Bear in mind that Decluttering constitutes building a comfortable environment that embodies the contemporary needs and wants of its occupants. **Encouragement:** For every step that is taken to clean up, clear things, and get rid of clutter, it is time to cherish the change and the opportunity for growth that comes with it. Buy less and own more – lose the things that don't add value to your life and find meaning in the things you have. It stated that if you let go of all these and leave space for it, you can have the optimal of everything, happiness, focus, and achievement.

Conclusion

Recap of Unique Challenges and Benefits: Senior citizens have certain issues that make the process very tickling like the psychological attachment of confining their personal property and the physical strength required to organize and sort through personal belongings. But there are definite advantages to living a life where one possesses only the barest essentials. Minimalism can also, therefore, make seniors' lives more ordered, peaceful, and meaningful. It makes everyone less stressed, improves focus and memory, and appears to make the house safer and even healthier. It also promotes things like relationships with family, and friends and enables one to prioritize and enhance what matters in life.

Encouragement to Embrace the Journey: There is nothing that I have discovered that is more of a process than decluttering and it is important that one has to be patient and have a sense of humor all through the process. It is advisable to embrace the process with self-compassion and be aware that every little act is a move forward. Then laugh at the difficulties and triumphs, however little they seem to be. As already mentioned, decluttering is not a flawless process that aims at the creation of a perfect environment to which you do not need to commit but the pursuit of a meaningful existence. That's when a person can attain a form of existence that is minimally complex and fully happy if he embraces this sort of trip.

Looking Forward to a Clutter-Free Life: Look ahead, people, to the serenity and happiness you will enjoy that result from a clean home free from clutter. I speak from experience and when you declutter and remove anything that does not need to be in your vicinity in the first place, you set yourself up nicely for optimum functionality and enjoyment of life. Decluttering's journey is about a life that is maximally ordered, calm, and, more importantly, authentic. Thank you for coming and receiving the challenge that lies ahead of you as you proceed in the journey to lead a minimalist life.

Chapter 11: DIY Storage Solutions: Creative Ideas for Organizing Clutter Effectively

Upcycling: Turning Trash into Treasure (or at Least Something Functional)

Introduction to Upcycling

Upcycling is about taking junk, that no longer serves its purpose, and transforming it into something new and useful. It also encodes a completely different meaning where, instead of trashing all the objects that are no longer deemed useful for their initial purpose, upcycling helps one repurpose them. They say this also assists in the preservation of the environment since just a little product is chucked beside the rubbish bin in the landfill. **Hint:** "Consider upcycling as an art form, it is almost like granting yourself a license to provide your room or home with ornaments that are not only original but also have a beneficial impact on nature." **Guidance:** Begin with, for example, one item that you are close to, have a favorite or one that needs redesigning. **Encouragement:** Again, as I mentioned before, upcycling is not about having it perfect at the end of the journey. Have fun and get as creative as you can when upcycling what you previously thought of as 'trash' – your house will be better for it.

Practical Upcycling Projects

Just as a useful item it can be useful to have practical upcycling projects that are engaging and creative. For instance, you can recycle a bashed mug that you once used for your coffee by turning it into an eye-catching planter for a succulent or recycle parts and accessories of a bicycle, and come up with an artistic lamp. These projects are also economical since having a new object is not needed since the old one is turned into a new product. **Prompt:** Always consider the question, "What can I do with this?" before throwing something away, you could find a new favorite item. **Guidance:** Remember it is not always possible to have all the projects to be successful, that is normal. 'Upcycling is still a form of learning, and each time you try to create something, you also learn.' **Encouragement:** If a concept is not perfect, then upcycling is imprecise, and that's okay: Be accepting of the experimentation. Regardless of the outcome, each project increases your chances of becoming an expert on repurposing and makes your home unique.

Family-Friendly Upcycling

Encouraging your children to take up upcycling is also a good experience pastime that is enjoyable to the entire family. Using scraps of colored paper to make an art coffee filter or recycling crayons to create new shapes talks to children about conservation and inventions. **Hint:** Suggest these projects as family art time – again children are fascinated to see how their projects evolve. **Guidance:** Take advantage of such occasions, to teach children the value of recycling, and how they can help save the environment. **Encouragement:** Not only does upcycling help to be creative but also creates a strong unity with the entire family. These projects are worth performing as they can teach a lot of lessons about being economical while at the same time making memories. Of course, there should be a goal to be precise, yet the goal of a joint practice is to have fun and master the missed concepts collectively. Enjoy the process as well as the time spent together as a family, knowing that you are creating a positive change in your home as well as in the environment.

Seasonal Upcycling

Upcycling can easily be done for every season and this means that your home adornments will always be up to date. For example, during the fall one can utilize the jars for holding candles which provides the necessary atmosphere in a living room. In spring, pallets can be converted into garden planters making a new appearance for your outdoor space. **Prompt:** Think about what other products you may have in stock for the current season that can be used for decoration purposes instead of having to buy more. **Guidance:** Other possible upcycling arts for different seasons ensure that creativity in upcycling is not limited by the amount of unused items that are bought throughout the year. **Encouragement:** With the approach of each next season, following the traditions of upcycling, you can dispose of unnecessary things, at the same time creating a cozy atmosphere responding to the current months in your home. Also, never underestimate digital revitalization: transform the past photos into vibrant digital calendars or photo albums, to give a new life to the memories and to bulk up digital collections. This practice is useful in ensuring that your physical and cyber worlds are ordered and significant.

Clever Storage Hacks: Making the Most of Every Nook and Cranny

Under-Bed Storage

Less space often lies under the bed and is the perfect place to store items such as clothes that are used in different seasons, extra cushioning, or even candies. These should be placed in under-bed bins to ensure the items are not displayed but can be accessed easily. **Hint:** Make sure that you label the bins so that whatever one you are looking for is easy to find. **Guidance:** That is, it is important not to create another mess simply as another place where the items had to be put. Less is more and it should serve the purpose for which it was designed. **Encouragement:** Under-bed storage is perfect for people with little space in their homes. They allow for effective utilization of space so, no part of the room goes to waste; all the items you own will have their rightful place on the shelves and you rarely see clutter around the house. This method of storage is excellent for small houses because it will help you eliminate the clutter and yet it will not be invasive or take up a lot of space.

Kitchen Storage Solutions

One of the many techniques of uncluttering is in the utilization of the kitchen area, especially the countertops. In cabinets, for example, Lazy Susans can be employed to make items easily accessible thus no need to reach for things from behind crowded shelves. Magnetic spice jars are another excellent example: those spice jars can be mounted on the fridge instead of occupying a lot of shelf space. **Prompt:** It is worthwhile to read this information before starting to organize your working space and remember that it is always useful to prioritize things and place them in areas that are easily accessible. **Guidance:** Make sure that the items stored in the pantry are well arranged by categories and placed in the bin with a clear label. This makes it easy to locate the item that one wants and helps in avoiding cases of redundancy in purchasing similar items. **Encouragement:** A clean and well-organized kitchen not only must be appealing to the eye, but they are also conducive to good meal preparation.

Vertical Storage for Kids' Rooms

Vertical storage is another good way to store things that children tend to litter their rooms with. If there are toys, shoes or other small items to be stored, over-the-door organizers can be used to get the most storage space without occupying the floor. The last is wall-mounted shelves – the accessories enable to free the space from toys and books, which simplifies cleaning and makes the hall more convenient. **Hint:** You also want to engage your children to decorate their storage in the kind of colors and accents they love. **Guidance:** Find ways how to make it easy for your child to label and organize their belongings so that they can easily remember the location of the items. **Encouragement:** Vertical storage also gives more space and also makes children learn that things have to be arranged in different order. That way you also assist in helping them develop habits that will keep their room tidy in the future, to top it up, you are creating an environment they will enjoy.

Digital Storage Hacks

Decluttering isn't just for physical spaces—your digital life needs attention too. The first step is to start cleaning by deleting those apps that are not in regular use, and by folding the files so that they are easily categorizable. Another important step is backing up photographs – guarantee that your priceless moments are protected and may be quickly restored. **Prompt:** One must always ask themselves questions like, do I need this app or this particular file or document before storing it? **Guidance:** This common habit of accumulating files can be easily solved by creating a system of classification that is comfortable for you – by the date, by categories, by types of projects, etc. This is the only way through which one can avoid the accumulation of the items in the future since they are now aware of the result of the accumulation of those items. **Encouragement:** The tidiness of your virtual space is as important as the tidiness of a house a flat or a room. Once you de-junk your devices, you save yourself from a lot of stress and make your digital life as good as it can get in terms of the amount of productivity and how much fun it is. A well-ordered digital space can also provide for reassurance and the ability to find crucial files when needed and that they are safe in a backup.

DIY Storage Solutions for Specific Areas

Living Room Storage

The living room can be thought of as the central living area in many homes, therefore this space must be kept neat. It is also possible to utilize space on walls and ceilings and get additional shelves in the form of constructions placed for example above doors or in blank corners of the walls. Items like ottomans with built-in storage or coffee tables with secret cubbies help stow things away and have obvious use at the same time. Useful containers such as beautiful boxes and baskets give elegance and convenience while preventing unnecessary mess from accumulating in a home's charm. **Hint:** Get used to perceiving every item of furniture as a possibility of a storage space. **Guidance:** Maximize vertical space and choose furniture pieces and storage units that affirm the residing room design. **Encouragement:** When you introduce these smart storage solutions, you are going to come up with a cozy and liberating living room ambiance that guarantees the best and most comfortable moments are spent with friends and loved ones.

Bedroom Storage

The bedroom should be organized and clean; thus, there should be no clutter in the room. The first step is to make systems for organizing clothes, shoes as well as accessories so that they do not complicate your search. Using corner space, under-bed drawers are ideal for storing seasonal wear or extra sheets, thereby putting the unused space to good use. A less traditional design is an addition of special shelves directly into the headboards; they can be used for storing books or other accessories and as an aesthetic addition. **Hint:** This suggests that you should place your most often used items in easily accessible sections and for the items that you use less frequently you should put in sections that are out of sight. **Guidance:** Try to take out some clothes and accessories from your closet often to maintain order in your bedroom. **Encouragement:** ClosetId It is significantly important to ensure that the bedroom is free from clutter as this will only affect your sleep and result in an uncomfortable start to the day.

Bathroom Storage

Bathrooms are generally small, but there are ideas on how to use every square inch most efficiently. Shelves that are installed above the toilet are a useful way to take advantage of height when, for instance, storing toilet items, towels, or ornaments. In your bathroom area, there should be cabinets and to ensure you have an easy time when cleaning or even applying a skincare product, ensure it has organizers. Also, hooks and racks on the partitions or the doors must be placed to fold the towels and bathrobes without occupying space. **Hint:** Think of what you use most often and place it where you will find it easier to use. **Guidance:** Often, help to pick a bathroom storage solution, which means that you should look at your bathroom from time to time and see if the storage is still convenient and not cluttered. **Encouragement:** With these basic storage techniques, your bathroom becomes conducive for use, meaning that your morning rush will be much easier.

Garage and Basement Storage

People often use garages as storage areas and basements for things that they rarely use, but in proper arrangement, the latter can be very helpful. It includes pegboards, tool racks, and other such equipment that allows easy visibility of tools and equipment and easy access to them. It is possible to label and stack some of the storage bins to ensure that it is easier to sort out seasonal clothes, sports equipment, or holiday accessories; thus, these areas should not turn into dumping zones. Although to increase storage you can use floor space as discussed above, to maximize the ceiling space you can fix overhead racks which will help you store large items thus freeing the floor space. **Hint:** Before storing any item, ensure it is well labeled in a bid to avoid having to forget about its existence after being put away. **Guidance:** Spend time organizing and creating categories of the items in the garage or basement so that the two areas can be put to good use instead of causing a nuisance. **Encouragement:** Having the garage or basement neat and clean apart from creating physical space frees up the mind as one can find what one needs whenever one needs it.

Sustainable Decluttering Tips

Purpose: To promote eco-friendly decluttering practices, this chart provides tips on how to dispose of items responsibly and sustainably.

Sustainable Decluttering Tips

Tip	Check
Donate: Gently used items to local charities, shelters, or community centers	[ ]
Recycle: Electronics, batteries, and other items through appropriate recycling programs	[ ]
Upcycle: Repurpose old items into something new and useful (e.g., turning an old ladder into a bookshelf)	[ ]
Compost: Organic materials like food waste and plant clippings instead of sending them to the landfill	[ ]
Sell: Items of value that you no longer need through online marketplaces or yard sales	[ ]
Repair: Fix broken items instead of discarding them if possible	[ ]
Minimize: Future waste by adopting a "buy less, choose well" mindset	[ ]

Eco-Friendly Disposal Methods

Item	Disposal Method	Check
Old Electronics	Take to an e-waste recycling facility	[ ]
Clothing	Donate to a clothing bank or charity	[ ]
Furniture	Sell, donate, or upcycle	[ ]
Books and Magazines	Donate to libraries, schools, or community centers	[ ]
Plastic Items	Recycle through appropriate local programs	[ ]
Glass and Metal	Recycle through curbside recycling or at local drop-off centers	[ ]
Food Waste	Compost or use in a garden	[ ]

Sustainable Decluttering Tips

Sustainable Shopping Practices

Practice	Check
Buy Less, Choose Well: Focus on quality over quantity to reduce waste	[ ]
Opt for Secondhand: Purchase secondhand or vintage items to minimize your environmental impact	[ ]
Support Sustainable Brands: Choose products from companies committed to sustainable practices	[ ]
Avoid Single-Use Items: Use reusable items like bags, water bottles, and containers	[ ]
Plan Purchases: Make a list before shopping to avoid impulse buys	[ ]
Repair Before Replacing: Consider fixing an item before buying a new one	[ ]

Final Sustainable Actions

Action	Check
Commit to sustainable decluttering and living	[ ]
Share your sustainable practices with friends and family	[ ]
Reflect on how these changes have positively impacted your life and the environment	[ ]
Continue to educate yourself about eco-friendly living	[ ]
Regularly review and update your sustainability goals	[ ]

Maintaining Your Clutter-Free Space

Regular Decluttering Sessions

Cleanliness is something that must be done daily to avoid building up clutter. In terms of the strategy of scheduling, try to find intervals that are convenient for you to declutter – for example, weekly, monthly, or seasonal, so that clutter has no chance to accumulate. Independent, fast cleaning can be carried out in several daily activities like, for instance, cleaning the kitchen before going to bed or the living room. Seasonal reviews give the flexibility of overhauling, as well as clearing up space since different seasons have different demands. **Hint:** If you feel overwhelmed just set a timer for fifteen minutes and look how much you will be able to organize—the small steps will make the difference. **Guidance:** Consistency is key. Scheduling sessions minimizes the buildup of clutter to the extent that encourages the subject to clean. **Encouragement:** If you are uncluttering your home and setting out some time each week to keep things neat, your home will be prepared to tackle anything that comes its way.

Mindful Consumption

Mindful consumption is one of the most effective routines for avoiding clutter growth in the home environment. Conduct consequent consumption thinking about intentional consumption and purchasing only those things that will be useful to you in a certain period. Do not use credit cards as a way of spending money, use time to think and ditch the credit card by asking yourself whether you need that product or if it will help you to be happy. **Hint:** Formulate a list of your desires in life and do not purchase anything on the list for at least a month. **Guidance:** Fashion the house with quality items only and whatever is inside the house should be meaningful to own. **Encouragement:** You avoid wasting money and creating a home full of purposeful items while at the same time avoiding items that only clutter up your home.

Involving the Whole Family

Decluttering is not something that should be done by individuals alone; they always should try to involve the entire family. Make a habit of organizing a family decluttering day where everybody contributes to cleaning and sorting things within the compound. Introducing children to the importance of tidiness and cleaning their spaces should not be done In a boring way but instead Should Inculcate fun and reward systems. To involve kids in decluttering, one can turn the process into a game or a kind of challenge. **Hint:** Rewards should be given in the form of small incentives or privileges when an assignment is done. **Guidance:** Regular engagement of the family makes everybody participate in the process of keeping the house clean and free. **Encouragement:** Group work not only maintains cleanliness at one's home but at the same time involves everybody and encourages cooperation.

Long-Term Benefits of a Clutter-Free Home

From decluttering one's home, clean up derives much more than a clean house. Savor the feeling of orderliness and serenity that is enjoyed in an office environment. As for increased productivity, it is all clear for a sensible person: you don't waste time looking for things that get lost because they are in order. Lastly, decluttering brings overall life quality when you get to make the best use of your home without having to deal with all those items. **Hint:** Think about the benefits that you have experienced as a result of decluttering your home. **Guidance:** To enjoy these benefits in the long also, ensure that you keep your surroundings free of clutter. **Encouragement:** Clutter renders it difficult to live a balanced life and do what one enjoys doing by taking up a lot of time and mental energy.

Conclusion

Recap of Strategies: The primary condition for free from clutter home is the existence of storage systems, as well as their proper usage and cleaning. Category: Flexible storage solutions; see: Artful storage, space-saving furniture, conscientious purchasing, and family collaborations Some of these strategies are creative storage accessories Multipurpose furniture Mindful buying, and Family participation When you are using these methods, you will be able to convert any section of the house into a practical visible and calming space.

Embracing Creativity and Fun: Uncluttering is not a task that one can bore oneself to death with. Be creative and do not be afraid to have as much fun cleaning up as you have while creating the mess; to clean up, try to make inventions, like a game. In my opinion, if you are happy to declutter, then this positive attitude will make it a normal chore like any other.

Looking Forward: General cleanliness of the home is associated with many broad advantages that ensure a positive bounce to people's well-being in the long run. This, along with making the conscious decision to declutter more often and to make wiser purchases, will bring into your life the environment that you want and will enjoy every day. Before you have the fascination of having a clean and well-organized home and this comes with disappointments and anxiety.

Chapter 12:
Conclusion: Embracing a Life of Less (And More Room for Joy)

Celebrating Your Decluttering Journey: You Did It!

Acknowledging Your Achievement

I want you to pause for a while and admire yourself for the wonderful journey you have accomplished. From the confusing mess that used to be your home to the clean order you have put in your home every step you have made requires appreciation. If organization and cleanliness are something you strive for, then the metaphor of a confetti party will make perfect sense: every flake is a victory, such as finding a threaded needle or putting the remote control on the proper shelf when you're done with it. **Hint:** Think of the times you have been triumphant one time or several times in your life. **Guidance:** Again, these are not mere accomplishments in the sphere of cleaning; they represent victory over chaos and, therefore, over one's own life. **Encouragement:** Accept the satisfaction of working and knowing that a home has been ordered and organized to suit the best person that you are.

Treating Yourself

Having carried out all these, you should allow yourself some sort of reward. Whether it is buying a slice of cake for dinner, getting a new plant for a clean, no longer cluttered house, or getting a magazine of the new minimalistic life, treat yourself. **Prompt:** Think to yourself, "What will help me savor this victory even more?" **Guidance:** Understand that, while decluttering, one frees not only the physical space but also their mind. As you decluttered, you also decluttered your mind: you found new and fresh energy to focus on the things left as well as new strength in yourself. **Encouragement:** Forcing oneself to stick to this new format of organizing is difficult, and by rewarding oneself, the positive feelings regarding decluttering are maintained.

Sharing Your Story

You should share your decluttering experience to help others, and you may have lots to share if you have been on the journey for a while. Take a 'before' photo and an 'after' photo and share the process on social media, write a blog, or even make a TikTok about the process. **Hint:** It is always inspiring for folks to see a change in real life—tell your story; there may be somebody out there who wants to start on a decluttering spree as well. **Guidance:** Do not censor the good the bad the insane and the tiny victories. Getting real takes the journey to the next level and inspires other people to go through the process with warts and all. **Encouragement:** Well, telling the story or being active on the blog, it's not a way to boast only, to show everybody that you are a successful person or you are good at organizing your life—you share the stories and become a part of a community of people who have the same aim—to live a simple life intentionally.

Appreciating Emotional Growth

Decluttering is not only rearranging things; it is a process of healing. That is the reason as you are giving away things, you are also giving away the sentiment behind the things that bind you to them: memories. **Prompt:** Think about the things you felt you had a wrenching time letting go of: what did you manage to understand about yourself and your current health status? **Guidance:** Sometimes it may be more important to note that you should take your time and look with horns of appreciation at the merits which have been learned and the growth which you have been able to undergo. Every single decision to let go or hold on depends on another step in the direction of defining what is important to you. **Encouragement:** Not only the space on the bed but the space in your minds and hearts which you cleared out and this is what needs to be celebrated. While I have been working on decluttering my home, I have gained as much as I have lost.

Moving Forward: Living a Life Filled with Purpose and Space

Crafting a Purposeful Life

After you have completed this process of sorting your items, it is now time to create the purpose of the available space. Design a house where people want to wake up and be happy, where every room is a reflection of your dreams. **Hint:** How would it be waking up to a clean, tidy house that is fully prepared to handle whatever comes its way? **Guidance:** Take advantage of the space you have created for ideas, appreciation, or expression and use it by creating a space for thoughts to grow such as creating a reading corner, an Art corner, or even a clean table where the ideas can develop. **Encouragement:** When a house is clean or uncluttered, it is not only pleasing to the eye, but it's the core of a well-ordered life. There is less to occupy your time and therefore you get to engage in what makes you happy.

Knowing What You Want

When advancing, maintain your focus on what is important, and reshape and develop your space according to your interests. It is good to detach oneself from items that are not useful and surround yourself with things that are meaningful to you. **Prompt:** You have to ask yourself, 'Does this ring any bell?', or 'Does this bring joy or help me achieve my goals?' **Guidance:** We are mostly known to have both a physical clutter and a mental one. This is because, by manipulation of the objects present in one's life, one ensures that only the surroundings that put the best version of themselves forward are around them. **Encouragement:** As I always note, your home is the first place that should inspire you every morning when you wake up. The idea is that the more purposeful the space is, the more harmonious one's life will be with what he or she wants.

Room-Specific Decluttering

Now that you have developed your skills, approach each room with a specific goal in mind. Organize your kitchen first, by sorting out spices in the kitchen, disposing of those that have passed their shelf life, and most importantly, rationalizing their placement as much as possible. Go to the living room, incorporating the "Less is More" philosophy, and get the most out of the stress-free environment. Last but not least minimize the clutter by removing anything that does not directly relate to sleep from your bedroom. **Hint:** Ensure that you do one room at a time so that one is not overwhelmed in the process. **Guidance:** There are several objectives that each room has in your life; thus, it would be best to organize it to improve its role. Encouragement: In this way, you will design the space with a purpose, and as a result, you will live in a beautiful home that also makes you feel good.

Family-Friendly Decluttering

Teach your children how to declutter entertainingly so that they will not get bored. challenges and fun for such and such to own up to the space for example, turning it and setting a few rules and regulations whereby they compete to clean up their area after you introduce the gauntlet. **Prompt:** Question your children, "What can we remove from our sight for today to pave the way for something new and more exciting?" **Guidance:** It has been found useful to teach children the essence of tidiness and cleanliness in the house to avoid cluttering and learning how to own responsibilities. **Encouragement:** Assign meaning to memories: Often the challenge is not in parting with things but in keeping track of instances that sparked the need for the items in the first place, for instance, take a picture of an item that is associated with a memorable event, as you keep the picture you eliminate the need for the physical object. Beyond that, it helps to alleviate the burden, which, in turn, enlightens children about some important aspects of life and improves their ability to cope with it

Maintaining Your Clutter-Free Space

Seasonal Decluttering

It is good to declutter seasonally especially when there is a change of season because this enables one to maintain order in the limited space all through. The minute that one season is up and another comes along, your requirements and necessities change with the objects you take with you. Seasonal clearances concern reviewing your possessions every one or two seasons with a view of determining what best fits this new season and dumping the unnecessary or unused items. For instance, when winter is approaching the end and summer replaces it, it is the best time to put away the summer outfits and look at the condition of the clothes, whether it is necessary to give them to someone or trash them. **Hint:** One of the smart approaches is to clean based on the change of seasons or time for new clothes and shoes, new books, new toys, etc. **Guidance:** A person should go on asking, "Have I used this during this particular season?" If their answer is negative, then it is high time they said adieu to the particular item. **Encouragement:** This way, you avoid the accumulation of things that are not needed at the moment, thus organizing your house to describe the state which will reflect a functional space, a sanctuary from the outside world.

Digital Decluttering

Clutter is not only physical but can also be digital due to the increased use of technology in our daily lives. Weekly 'digital spring clean' is very necessary for sorting out files, applications, and photographs that one downloads or clicks in a month. Minimizing the complexity of your digital tools is almost certain to minimize distractions and improve productivity or efficiency. It is advisable to pick a recurring schedule every month to dedicate a certain amount of time to doing an audit of your digital environment. **Hint:** Schedule a clean-out for a "Digital declutter day." **Tip:** When looking at a particular application or a file, always ask yourself "Does this application or file have any usefulness in my life?" If it does not have, get rid of it. **Encouragement:** Cleaning up digital clutter has nothing to do with the physical clean up of physical space in your devices, it is a process of coring out mental space. A healthy digital life minimizes the sources of tension and keeps you on track so that technology can be used in a positive way, not in a way that creates overwhelm.

Mindful Consumption

One has to be conscious while buying items that would help avoid cluttering the house. Consciously, selecting items of necessity guarantees that every item you get into your house adds value to your life. It is good to take a short break before purchasing something new, then ask yourself if it is useful, or if it was a whim. **Hint:** Use a 'cooling-off' period – do not purchase without waiting 24 hours. **Guidance:** Some of the things include, asking yourself if the item that you are buying will still be useful to you after a few days or months by asking yourself Questions like is this going to be useful to me in the future? **Encouragement:** Besides avoiding clutter, mindful consumption also means that a person only spends money on things he or she needs or wants. Working this way, you will observe that you possess relatively fewer things, yet are content with what you have. Intentionality is the part of this approach that I like most; because in this way one feels in control of the environment and therefore ends up surrounding oneself with things that are full of value as opposed to objects that are just cluttering up the space.

Long-Term Benefits

Sustainable decluttering is rewarding in the long run as it has significant impacts on the lives of individuals. Donating, recycling, and upcycling are some of the ways through which you can embrace sustainable practices hence creating a sustainable life. These are not just mere cleaning activities but help inculcate the spirit of responsibility and being careful. **Hint:** The golden rule should be asked more often, 'Can this item be donated or recycled?' **Guidance:** Small changes in the daily routine will ensure that a house does not get messy and cluttered within a short span. **Encouragement:** Living in such a clean environment has its privileges and creating a wrinkled world is one of them. It also fosters intentionality and peace hence making your home a haven. Gradually, these practices change the way you relate to material things, and life itself, as well as the way you construct your existence that will be efficient, uncluttered, and harmonious.

Embracing the Minimalist Mindset

Joy of Less

Minimalism is not just the act of getting rid of items; it is the refusal to own things which doesn't make us happy. Instead of qualities that will gradually perish with cathedrals, you invest in values which People and relationships, opportunities, and personal development make up a meaningful life. **Hint:** Think about the moments in life that make you happy, more often the happiness is connected to some events or people. **Guidance:** One of the questions that you should ask yourself is, 'Does the item contribute to the kind of life I wish to live?' It assists in identifying what matters most. **Encouragement:** Another advantage of minimalism is that it helps people to be relieved from the constant influence of the necessity to buy more and more things. But it compels you to wish for less than you already have, to rediscover joy within limited means. This not only has the advantage of getting rid of stuff that you do not need, and therefore getting rid of physical clutter, but also works on the mind and the heart, bringing a more satisfying and happy life.

Humor and Imperfection

Decluttering is not just about getting to a certain endpoint but more about movement and having fun while at it. Accept the occasional jokes and mistakes that are bound to happen—remember, the real world is not as clean as the dogmatism, and neither is the task of sorting it out. **Hint:** It is funny when sifting through the piles of clothes and other possessions; embrace the crazed laughter because it can happen to anyone. **Guidance:** Tell yourself that's not a sin for things to go wrong. Progress is what matters. **Encouragement:** Empower the space with a pop-up to 'A thank you for the efforts made rather than congratulations for the job done well'. Juvenile chatter is just one of the things that disappear when one steps into this office, and enjoying the liberty it offers is worth the entry. But dear readers, the concept of 'home' is not about impeccable aesthetics, it is more about designing a house that truly fits and brings comfort and joy to the inhabitants' lives, as they are.

Setting Future Goals

Organization of the space free of clutter means thinking about the future. Setting aside one's time to declutter the home and one's life is imperative and should be conducted periodically throughout the seasons and in the digital platforms we use. **Hint:** Have finite goals for each decluttering session like, 'Clean the closet' or 'Sort the photo collection'. **Directions:** The advice is as follows - choose the question from the following – 'What micro-steps can I take today for maintaining a decluttered space?' **Encouragement:** There can always be room for improvement and thus this calls for constant improvement; this idea holds ground. Age as well as stage is also an important consideration because as your life changes your requirements also change. Continuously optimize your surroundings and the environment you live in as much as possible to reflect the set goals and their values. When you adopt new goals about what you want your home to be in the days and months to come and when you practice routine cleaning and clearing, you keep distilling your home to the function of helping you become the more intentional person you want to be.

Looking Forward

When transitioning into a more organized lifestyle free from clutter, expect a new future of opportunities that are available to you. With less clutter and fewer things vying for attention, you have time for the things that matter to you, such as a passion, family, or a clean home. **Hint:** Try to imagine how liberating it is to truly live without clutter – it is not just about the absence of material things, but the presence of opportunities. **Guidance:** You may also want to pose the question "What can I do with this extra space that may bring more positive aspects in my life?" This questioning encourages the generation of new ideas. **Encouragement:** While at it, do not fail to relish the gains, and the freedom that you have attained. Toast to the bliss of minimalism and welcome the opportunities that come with frugal living and decluttered home. This journey is not just about organizing; it is about stepping into a life organically yours, a life that is fulfilling and meaningful.

Conclusion

Recap of the Journey: Congratulations on the new attitude, which you brought with you while decluttering as well as on the changed space. Well done – by decluttering, you've managed to turn your home into the place that you truly are on the inside: orderly, calm, and purposeful. Hint: If you found yourself in this position, then think about how far you have evolved. Guidance: If there is any assistance that will be useful in improving your experience of decluttering, remember the relief felt when you were able to free yourself from clutter. Encouragement: It helps to take stock of your victories no matter how little or small they are since everything you do is advancing you to the life that you want; the uncomplicated life that you desire.

Encouraging Continual Growth: The road map does not stop here. Maintain the following adoration of minimalism and then some: Hint: Someone once said, 'The World is not made for the likes of me,' so continue to invent means of making your life less complex. Guidance: Always ask yourself – 'What can I polish up to the next level?' Greatness: Keep improving and never stop developing as a person with the help of minimalism to build a life that is clean and full of depth and happiness.

Anticipating the Future: Stand before the future with passion, prepared with the idea that minimalism has the potential to alter your life. Hint: Try to picture a life you desire and which does not have to carry so much weight. Guidance: Keep your eyes on the prize and be aware that elaboration of thought leads to not happiness. Encouragement: Capture the opportunities that they bring and have fun for the journey to a happier, less cluttered, and more satisfying life.

Chapter 13: The Minimalist Mindset: Cultivating a Life of Intentionality and Joy

Understanding the Minimalist Mindset

Defining Minimalism

Minimalism is not only about removing stuff from one's life, but it's also a principle-guided way of living. Notably, it motivates you to declutter not only your environment but also your life in general. Minimalism embraces three dominant principles, namely the principles of simplification, purposeful, and purposeful consciousness all aiming to help you make the right decisions. This shift can make you get the point of what matters, help to lessen stress, enhance the ability to concentrate, and in the end, increase the level of happiness. **Hint:** In my opinion, one can consider minimalism as decluttering the mind and the environment it exists in. **Guidance:** Better begin by recognizing spheres of life in which you experience stress. Would you like to bring less stress to your life by modifying these areas? **Encouragement:** Learning how to live with less is not about depriving one's self; it is about being able to find and create space for happiness, simplicity, and serenity in one's life.

Shifting Perspectives

Having a minimal mentality merely informs you that you need to be wise and keen with all aspects one gets into. It is the awareness that possessing 'as much as needed' is more rewarding than possessing 'as much as possible'. The Machete perspective interferes with this concept that holds that the more one acquires, the more clutter he accumulates, be it physically or in his mind.

Prompt: Making the question to yourself "Do I need this or is it just a coping mechanism?" can make you have enough which in turn, can lead to happiness. **Guidance:** Make an evaluation of objects, which you possess and the values, self-fulfillment, and satisfaction you pursue. Are they improving your existence, or are they just occupying your time and making it appear as though you're productive? **Encouragement:** As you learn to let go of the desire to possess material items you can pursue the things that give you more fulfillment such as experience, people, and growing as an individual.

Mindful Decision-Making

One of the strategies of minimalism is the conscious choice in favor of what is important to a person and what they want to achieve. Whenever you think about purchasing something new, remind yourself again, 'Do I need it?' It is a question that will assist you in not bringing unnecessary stuff into your home. **Hint:** Just think about what specific part of your lives these new things are going to add before you bring it home. **Guidance:** Make a 'hearts and minds' list, or a 'pen and paper' list, of what matters most to you, and keep these in mind when you make choices. **Encouragement:** Living with purpose also means not being influenced by demands that do not influence improving one's life. Organizational culture will help you to adapt values to choices so that there will be more meaning, and more purpose, in what would otherwise be small, mundane decisions.

Creating a Minimalist Environment

Minimizing items in your home and 'decluttering' your living space by adhering strictly to minimalist principles is good for the body, mind, and soul. Care should be taken to ensure that initial creation involves designing environments that call for minimizing the use of force. Simplify – less is more – select pieces that are both practical and appealing to the eye. It has been seen that in this type of environment motifs and objects both functional and decorative exist in harmony. **Prompt:** Just as we need to ask, "Does this object bring me peace?" you might want to start wondering, "Does this space bring me peace?" **Guidance:** Concentration should be made on the fact that there should be no distractions on the walls and the colors used should be serene. **Encouragement:** Minimalism is not only about the looks of a house; it is about the environment that can encourage or help one to unwind due to the lack of things that are not necessary.

Building Minimalist Habits

Daily Routines

Experiencing a minimalist day starts with creating everyday habits that will make you embrace the minimalist culture. Habitual practices like mindful walking or having tea in the morning have the net effect of grounding a person. Evening wind-down processes put you in a position to let go of the day's stress most easily by preparing the body for sleep. Taking a mindful break during one's working hours is a way of anchoring oneself. **Hint:** Begin with baby steps, which shouldn't be more than waking up in the morning and doing one mindful practice. **Guidance:** Select those that have the biggest meaning to you and will allow you to stay more minimalist in between the waking hours. **Encouragement:** Proactivity has already been mentioned but structuring your day so that the day-to-day tasks you do are simple provides a very natural way of reclaiming your time from the chaos.

Sustainable Practices

It is an important thing to achieve to adopt as many aspects of sustainability into your routine as possible when practicing minimalism. Select options and products that would be environmentally friendly and minimize on wastage of resources. Simply shopping less and shopping smart-meaning to buy things that are essential and bought from environmentally responsible stores, can help in eradicating clutter. **Prompt:** Whenever you have to purchase an item, think twice and say to yourself, "Is this useful?" or "Was this product made using sustainable materials?" Recycling and reusing are also core principles of minimalism. **Guidance:** The best way of hitting this mark is by taking a long-term vision of the carbon footprint you are going to generate and, therefore, try and minimize it when making your purchase. **Encouragement:** Every piece of advice and every conscious act towards green is a part of the big picture of sustainable living and the positive effect we intend to take.

Mindful Consumption

Consumption of minimalism is key. Think through acquiring new things and make sure that these things will be useful to you and not just useless stuff. The principles of digital minimalism like setting time limits to screen time, or choosing content wisely, make you think less and focus more. Try 'unplugging' from social networks – it must be quite useful at times to just log out and listen to yourself. **Hint:** Reduce your device usage and note the impact on your headspace immediately. **Guidance:** Unplug from your digital activities and try to put in place new strategies that will help you achieve your minimalist goals. **Encouragement:** But, when you eat consciously, you make room for those things that would otherwise be overshadowed by the constant array of insignificant concerns.

Maintaining Minimalism

There must be several check-ins regularly to assess the practices that will support the concept of minimalist living. It is therefore important to time change and implement new and improved minimalistic looks because the seasons offer excellent chances to reconsider space and practices employed. Join the minimalist groups to get the kind of motivation and help to keep on track as desired. **Prompt:** Consider each of the four seasons: What aspects of home and life need a 'less is more' approach? **Guidance:** You can schedule some time of the day and dedicate it to such check-ins to avoid the accumulation of clutter. **Encouragement:** Keeping things simple is not a process that happens in one setting, maintaining such order is a process. Thus, by remaining consistent, you will be able to maintain an incredible experience of life being purposeful and meaningful.

Mindfulness Prompts for Decluttering

Purpose: To encourage a mindful approach to decluttering, this chart includes prompts that help you focus on the emotional and psychological aspects of letting go.

Mindfulness Prompts for Decluttering

Prompt	Check
How does this item make me feel when I see or use it?	[ ]
Is this item adding value to my life, or is it just taking up space?	[ ]
Am I holding onto this item out of fear, guilt, or habit?	[ ]
Does this item align with the person I am today or the person I want to be?	[ ]
Would I miss this item if it were gone, or would I feel relieved?	[ ]
Can I honor the memory associated with this item in another way (e.g., a photo or journal entry)?	[ ]
What does this item represent to me, and why is it hard to let go?	[ ]

Mindfulness Decluttering Practices

Practice	Check
Take a deep breath before making decisions about each item	[ ]
Pause and reflect on how each item impacts your mental space	[ ]
Express gratitude for items that have served their purpose	[ ]
Visualize your ideal space and how each item fits into it	[ ]
Practice letting go with a sense of peace and acceptance	[ ]
Focus on the present moment and how decluttering will improve your life	[ ]
Use mindful breathing to stay calm and centered during the process	[ ]

Mindfulness Prompts for Decluttering

Reflection Questions

Question	Check
How has decluttering impacted my mental clarity and well-being?	[ ]
What emotions arise when I think about letting go of certain items?	[ ]
How can I use this experience to cultivate a more mindful approach to life?	[ ]
What have I learned about myself through the process of decluttering?	[ ]
How will I continue to apply mindfulness in my daily life moving forward?	[ ]

Actionable Steps

Action	Check
Apply mindfulness to every aspect of your decluttering process	[ ]
Take time to reflect on your progress and the emotions that arise	[ ]
Incorporate mindfulness practices into your daily routines	[ ]
Let go of items with a sense of gratitude and closure	[ ]
Continue to cultivate a mindful, clutter-free lifestyle	[ ]

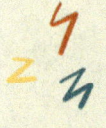

Minimalism and Relationships

Simplifying Social Life

While people live in a world of endless commitments, trimming down your social circle makes room for more substantial friendships. Instead of having a large number of weak ties, which can lead to meaningless connections and do not make one happy, it is better to get a few close friends and have friendly or friendly-love relationships which do make one happy and make one content. What this means is that you are very selective with the activities you engage in socially so that you only get involved with activities that indeed make you a happier person. Boundaries matter here, do not agree to attend or engage in things that bring you down, and avoid those that bring out the best in you. **Hint:** Try to do a reality check look at the present list of social engagements and ask the question, "Which are the activities that interest me?" **Guidance:** Cut down on basic social engagements and work more to improve the quality of time spent on meaningful relationships. **Encouragement:** This process of singling down your social circle not only saves time but also improves the quality of your actual relations.

Family and Minimalism

Minimalism is not only an individual practice: it can serve as a way for building family values and having the same vision. Sometimes, family practices must be adjusted to the principles of the minimalist lifestyle so that all members of the family realize that they live not for possessions but for purpose. Educational work for children and their parents and the use of examples of minimalism create lifetime habits of prudence and appreciation. Involve your family in carrying out group cleaning endeavors—tidying up your home helps to lessen the burden and make the family stronger. **Prompt:** Get your family's input using this question, "What should we keep for ourselves, and what should we give up together?" **Direction:** Minimally take an approach of involving as many family members as possible in the cause of creating and maintaining order and cleanliness at home. **Encouragement:** There is much emphasis put on adopting the minimalist lifestyle as a family because the levels of support increase, and the unneeded are eliminated.

Minimalism in Friendships

Minimalism can also improve friendships since it promotes healthy support and the replacement of the same values. Remind your friends about the articles and recommend how to implement a minimalist lifestyle to them and ask them to do the same. Organise get-togethers that are less about following the themes of minimalism – purposeful interaction instead of obsessing over the arrangements. Such austere events can call for a potluck dinner or a casual walk in the park; the focus here is not on getting and spending but on fellowshipping. **Hint:** When thinking about a party or any other get-together, there are two questions that you need to ask yourself: "How can I turn this into a good event instead of a Diva night?" **Guidance:** Here it is good to note that your friends may have arrived at minimalism through different paths and therefore try to come up with values that are acceptable to everyone.

Minimalist Celebrations

Celebrations don't have to be extravagant to be meaningful. Minimalist celebrations often bring people closer by focusing on the true essence of the occasion. Plan simple, thoughtful gatherings that emphasize connection over excess. Explore gift-giving alternatives, such as sharing experiences or creating handmade items, which carry more sentimental value than store-bought goods. During holidays, practice mindfulness by focusing on the spirit of the celebration rather than getting caught up in consumerism. Prompt: Before your next celebration, ask yourself, "What is the true meaning of this occasion, and how can I honor it simply?" Guidance: Consider how you can simplify your celebrations without losing the joy and significance they bring. Encouragement: By embracing minimalist celebrations, you not only reduce stress and clutter but also create more meaningful and memorable experiences with your loved ones.

Sustaining a Minimalist Lifestyle

Continual Growth

Minimalism is more of a process that requires effort throughout one's life, and not just a goal to be attained a one point in time. Take it as a best practice to learn through the budding years and into your elderly digs to sharpen and improve on minimalism. Do not be too rigid with your minimalist journey, because it has to adjust to the changes that occur in one's life. Take it as a method of self-improvement and self-actualization so that you can consider only the core things in life. **Hint:** Remember to always be asking "How can I make today more minimalist?" **Guidance:** It is useful to think about your minimalist journey in general from time to time and then change certain things to fit your new goals and requirements of your life. **Encouragement:** Always bear in mind that minimalism is a very subjective process, perhaps one of the least prescriptive or proscriptive kinds of self-improvement there is. The idea is simply to keep on extending oneself, stepping forward, and broadening oneself so that the minimalist way of living remains relevant and useful.

Incorporating Minimalism into All Areas of Life

When people hear the word 'minimalism,' they think of having less stuff in their homes, but it can also be applied to each day. In your working life, austerity is the key to improving the quality and quality of work by bringing together only the necessary. In health and wellness, the application of minimalism should be woven together holistically, recommending practices that are both effective and healthy. When it comes to leisure and hobbies, choose what you believe in and enjoy and that will not add chaos to your life. **Prompt:** One may ask 'How can I implement minimalism at work? In my health? In my hobbies?' **Hint:** Find the possibilities of how we can decrease the complexity of many aspects of our lives while trying to follow through with the principles of minimalism. **Encouragement:** Thus, by applying minimalism in your life, work, relations, or hobbies, you design a harmonious, purposive, and worthwhile life.

Minimalism and Community

Building a minimalist community can provide support and inspiration on your journey. Engage with like-minded individuals to share experiences, challenges, and successes. Participate in community projects that promote simplicity and sustainability, such as neighborhood clean-ups or clothing swaps. Sharing your minimalist journey and knowledge with others can inspire positive change, encouraging a broader movement towards intentional living. Hint: Ask yourself, "How can I contribute to my community in a way that aligns with my minimalist values?" Guidance: Seek out or create opportunities to connect with others who share your commitment to minimalism, fostering a supportive and inspiring community. Encouragement: By engaging with a minimalist community, you not only strengthen your practice but also contribute to a collective effort towards a simpler, more sustainable world.

Looking Ahead

As you continue your minimalist journey, set future goals that reflect your values and aspirations. Embrace change as a natural part of growth, continually seeking ways to simplify and enrich your life. Focus on living a life filled with joy, purpose, and intentionality, guided by the principles of minimalism.

Prompt: Regularly ask yourself, "What are my long-term goals, and how can minimalism help me achieve them?" Guidance: Keep your focus on the bigger picture, using minimalism as a tool to create a life that truly reflects your values and desires. Encouragement: Looking ahead with a minimalist mindset, you can anticipate a future filled with clarity, happiness, and fulfillment, where every choice you make is intentional and aligned with your deepest values.

Conclusion

Recap of the Minimalist Journey: The minimalist journey is about more than just decluttering—it's a mindset shift that brings clarity, intentionality, and joy to every aspect of life. By focusing on what truly matters, you create space for deeper connections, personal growth, and meaningful experiences. The benefits of minimalism extend far beyond a tidy home; they encompass mental clarity, emotional peace, and a greater sense of purpose.

Encouragement for Sustained Minimalism: Embracing minimalism is a lifelong commitment, one that requires dedication and joy. Continue to simplify, refine, and adapt your practices, always keeping your values at the forefront. Remember, minimalism is not about perfection but about progress. Each small step towards simplicity is a victory, bringing you closer to a life that resonates with your true self.

Looking Forward to a Minimalist Future: As you move forward, look ahead to a future filled with intentionality, clarity, and happiness. Minimalism empowers you to live with purpose, free from the distractions of excess. By embracing this mindset, you open the door to a life where every decision is made with intention, leading to a deeper sense of fulfillment and joy. Encouragement: The journey ahead is bright—filled with the possibilities that come from living simply and intentionally. Embrace it with enthusiasm, and let minimalism guide you toward a life of greater meaning and happiness.

Chapter 14: Minimalist Practices for Everyday Life: Simplify to Thrive

Simplifying Daily Routines

Streamlining Morning Routines

Begin with the end in mind; create a simple morning practice that allows for a positive outlook. Stick to the basic needs to be addressed such as; waking up, making your bed, taking breakfast, and what you intend to do for the rest of the day. This gives you a clear state of direction and hence you can avoid confusion in the morning which enables you to set with the right attitude. There are daily reminders that should be necessarily included in one's schedule – a few minutes of meditation or writing a journal where one has to set one's focus for the day. **Hint:** The following are some ways in which one can simplify their morning routine; Wearing clothes has never been easier than preparing them the previous night or having a standard meal. **Guidance:** However, one must maintain a certain level of structure while being able to modify one's schedule to accommodate their needs. **Encouragement:** I have found that by having your day planned out in such an order, the rest of your day follows suit and is productively as well as peacefully planned out.

Efficient Meal Planning

As already mentioned, meal planning does not have to be very formal. It is advisable to use a minimal use of ingredients to prepare healthy meals for they take very little time. Center your attention on vitamins-rich dishes that may be repeatable several times a week. Ensure you maintain your kitchen clean and free from unnecessary items to make the work of preparation easier – this includes organizing your pantry shelves and your fridge. **Prompt:** Contemplate, "What's one meal this week I can make easier?" **Advice:** Look to do some meal prepping or cooking in advance to not stress about it during the heavier weeks. **Encouragement:** Instead of a complex diet, a minimalistic one is also effective in minimizing stress besides time and financial costs; this way you will spend more time with your families and friends rather than in the kitchen.

Organizing Workspaces

The dirty and cluttered environment will distract you and reduce your efficiency on the job. Create a simplistic environment at the workplace without having to incorporate many items and or accessories. Then, ensure you clear your desk and manage your working items well so that only those, that are necessary, are placed around the desk. Discuss how one should keep their files clean and free of clutter in a secure manner also keep a clean space, both physically and virtually. **Hint:** Do not clutter your desk with any items that you do not need regularly: bare space is as valuable as any other space. **Guidance:** Weekly maintenance – schedule to review the positions and organization of the workspace. **Encouragement:** Effective organization of the working area not only increases productivity but also allows to find the necessary balance of work and rest, thereby decreasing stress levels and increasing work efficiency. If you keep your workplace deliberately free from distraction and clutter, you will soon discover you can work with far greater efficiency.

Evening Wind-Down

Establishing a calming evening routine is key to unwinding and preparing for restful sleep. Focus on intentional activities that help you relax, such as reading, taking a warm bath, or practicing gentle stretches. Limit screen time before bed to avoid overstimulation and promote better sleep quality. Reflective practices like gratitude journaling can also foster a sense of peace as you end your day. **Prompt:** Ask yourself, "What can I do tonight to ensure a restful sleep?" Guidance: Consider creating a bedtime ritual that you look forward to each evening. **Encouragement:** By dedicating time to unwind intentionally, you'll improve your sleep and wake up feeling refreshed, ready to embrace the new day with a clear and rested mind.

Minimalism in Personal Care and Wellness

Simplified Self-Care

Here is what I have learned about self-care – it does not have to be fancy. Concentrate on some core activities that are helpful for your personal development and do not take too much of your time. Choose a simple skincare regime using only the best and most versatile skin care products that serve different functions. Try habitually practicing meditation techniques that you can use in controlling relaxation stress levels while also improving your concentration. **Hint:** First of all, begin with organizing the bathroom, and get rid of products that you do not use daily. **Guidance:** Sort out an individual for those self-care practices that positively impact your life and discard the rest. **Encouragement:** Keeping positive fair approaches to self-care, lets you adhere to a specific schedule that would not become overwhelming to follow through the daily practice of managing health.

Wellness Through Minimalism

Engage yourself in a healthier lifestyle by adopting lifestyle changes that can improve your physical, psychological, and emotional status. Focus on simple exercises, for which you need little or no equipment and very little time, and which come with a lot of bang for your buck. Choose a different lifestyle that is free of processed food and adopt a balanced dietary culture. **Prompt:** Thinking on this, ask yourself, "What can I cut out from my wellness regimen to further enhance the wellness experience?" The answer is to follow the path of joy and what would nourish the body. **Encouragement:** Therefore, when you apply simple wellness practices, this creates a sustainable pattern that can be observed for the long-term hence healthy and happy individuals.

Mental Well-Being

Importantly, a minimalist lifestyle involves the kind of practices that maintain and enhance the health of one's mind. Be mindful and meditate because stress decreases and mental performance increases. Some forms of internal clutter are negative thoughts, resentments, or grudges, and eliminating these thoughts from your mind will also assist in the establishment of controlled positivity. Make an effort to balance work and play realizing that some time to just chill is as good as getting down to work. **Hint:** Spare some time to do some yoga or at least take some time performing deep breathing. **Guidance:** Incidentally, try to stop and examine yourself, checking in on your emotional and mental health. **Encouragement:** Minimalism for mental health barely suggests that you have to aim for the most important things in context to your health resulting in a calmer life.

Minimalist Fashion and Grooming

Simplify your wardrobe and grooming routines by focusing on quality over quantity. Create a capsule wardrobe with versatile, timeless pieces that reflect your style, making it easier to choose outfits each day. Streamline your grooming routine with essential, high-quality products that cover all your needs. Make conscious fashion choices, prioritizing sustainable and ethical brands that align with your values. **Prompt:** Ask yourself, "What are the essential items that truly represent my style?" **Guidance:** Start by decluttering your closet and keeping only what you love and wear regularly. **Encouragement:** By adopting a minimalist approach to fashion and grooming, you not only save time and reduce stress but also align your choices with a more sustainable and intentional lifestyle.

Decluttering Decision Tree

Purpose: A visual tool designed to help make quick and confident decisions about whether to keep, donate, or discard an item during the decluttering process.

Decluttering Decision Tree

Question	Decision Path	Action	Check
Do I use this item regularly?	**Yes:** Keep it and ensure it has a designated spot.	Keep and organize	[ ]
	No: Move to the next question.		
Is this item in good condition?	**Yes:** Consider if it brings value or joy.	Keep or donate	[ ]
	No: Move to the next question.		
Does this item bring me joy?	**Yes:** Keep it as part of your life.	Keep and organize	[ ]
	No: Move to the next question.		
Would I buy this item again today?	**Yes:** Keep it, but reassess its place in your home.	Keep or relocate	[ ]
	No: Move to the next question.		
Can this item be repurposed or donated?	**Yes:** Donate or repurpose to benefit someone else.	Donate or upcycle	[ ]
	No: If it's broken or no longer useful, discard it responsibly.	Recycle or discard	[ ]

When to Keep an Item

Condition	Check
It's used regularly and serves an important purpose	[ ]
It's in good condition and brings joy or value	[ ]
It's irreplaceable or holds significant sentimental value	[ ]
It's a high-quality item that fits with your lifestyle or decor	[ ]
It's a versatile item that serves multiple functions	[ ]

Decluttering Decision Tree

When to Donate or Repurpose an Item

Condition	Check
It's in good condition but no longer serves you	[ ]
Someone else could benefit from its use	[ ]
It can be upcycled into something more useful or attractive	[ ]
Is it a duplicate or do you have something better that serves the same purpose?	[ ]
It doesn't fit your current lifestyle, but it's still valuable	[ ]

When to Discard an Item

Condition	Check
It's broken beyond repair	[ ]
It's expired or unsafe to use	[ ]
It no longer functions or is obsolete	[ ]
It holds negative associations or no longer reflects who you are	[ ]
It's a single-use item that you no longer need or use	[ ]

Minimalism in Social and Leisure Activities

Intentional Socializing

While society is known for going big and wide, minimalism is likely to make you emphasize few but close relationships as against having many casual acquaintances. One must properly allocate the time with the people he or she deems worthy of spending time and effort with. When choosing hobbies and activities and when choosing your friends and company, be wise and make sure that what you are doing and who you are with mirrors what you believe in. The latter is also true about the restrictions and prohibitions that are also necessary to indicate. Take timely lessons on managing your time and energy so that you will be in a position to reject any other activity that is not healthy for you. **Hint:** Stand and think about, "Does this interaction help me to become who I want to become?" **Encouragement:** By being selective in your social life, you open a space to have good, healthy relationships and experiences leading to feelings of belonging and purpose.

Minimalist Hobbies

Opting for hobbies that could bring joy and relaxation is one of the major principles of the minimalist lifestyle. More effective are those tasks for which you won't need many supplies or big space, for instance, reading, doing yoga, or gardening. These are hobbies that offer much satisfaction and also do not result in the enhancement of clutter. Reducing the accumulation of material goods means going for pleasures that do not involve acquiring more stuff. Write, paint, or listen to music – such activities help in the expression of emotions and are very fulfilling without having to accumulate physical possessions. **Guidance:** Consider what brings you real joy and how your interests fit, or don't fit, into the minimalist view. **Encouragement:** Just remember it should not become some sort of obsession, that is the last thing any hobby should ever be, it shouldn't become a source of clutter and stress. What it turns into is asking yourself, "Is this a hobby that I derive happiness out of doing, or is it just another thing that must be completed on my schedule?"

Travel and Minimalism

Minimalism can transform the way you travel, making the experience more enjoyable and less stressful. Start by adopting minimalist packing strategies—bring only what you truly need, focusing on versatility and essentials. This approach not only lightens your load but also frees you to enjoy the journey without the burden of excess baggage. Embrace experiential travel by prioritizing experiences over souvenirs. Instead of filling your suitcase with trinkets, fill your heart with memories. Plan your trips with intention, choosing destinations and activities that align with your values. **Hint:** Before packing, ask, "Do I need this, or can I do without it?" **Encouragement:** Traveling light and mindfully allows you to focus on the essence of your journey—connecting with new places and people in a way that is meaningful and enriching.

Entertaining with Minimalism

Entertaining doesn't have to be extravagant to be memorable. Hosting simple, meaningful gatherings that emphasize connection over excess can be both fulfilling and stress-free. Focus on what truly matters: good company, good conversation, and a comfortable atmosphere. Plan minimalist parties with thoughtful touches, like using handmade decorations or serving homemade food, to create a warm and inviting environment. Sharing experiences and moments with loved ones rather than material gifts strengthens relationships and creates lasting memories. **Guidance:** When planning an event, ask, "How can I simplify this while making it special?" **Encouragement:** Remember, it's the connections and shared experiences that leave a lasting impression, not the things you accumulate. Simplifying your gatherings allows you to focus on what truly matters—celebrating togetherness in a meaningful way.

Sustaining Minimalist Practices

Building Long-Term Habits

One must remain consistent in maintaining a minimalist lifestyle if it is to be made and continued in the long run. For example, the deployment of each day as well as every week routines that entail simplification activities such as decluttering, and consuming in moderation. Introspection—useful in analyzing what is going well, what is not going well, and what changes you should prepare to make. They work to ensure that your practices remain in line with those things that are becoming increasingly important to you. Don't get rigid and stuck to a way of thinking as minimalism as a concept isn't set in stone and doesn't apply to everyone. But it is all about what has been found to best suit a given phase of life. **Prompt:** You need to ask yourself questions like, "What habits have been beneficial to me?" **Encouragement:** With time, one develops steady habits and is willing to change so that they keep on embracing minimalism throughout their lives to get lasting fulfillment and calmness.

Minimalism in Different Life Stages

Minimalism is not a state of stagnation, but a form of existence that a person undergoes at one time or another in one's life. When you want to shift, for instance, from being a student to a working person or from being a bachelor to a married man or a father, minimalism can assist you in making these changes. During these shifts, it is best to think of essentialism that will help you cut through the noise and discard what is unnecessary. Finally, in later life, minimalism helps in the simplification of the places that you live in to ensure they are comfortable to live in. **Guidance:** Consider the potential in which minimalism can help you in each life stage. **Encouragement:** As always, it is essential to recall that minimalism does not equal lack; it means having a life that corresponds to your present-stage existential priorities. In old age, the concept of 'less is more' which depicts the life of a less complicated and more fulfilling life should be embraced.

Community and Minimalism

Engaging with like-minded individuals and communities can strengthen your commitment to minimalism. Share support, ideas, and inspiration with others on a similar journey. Advocate for minimalist principles within your community, promoting sustainable and intentional living through your actions and words. Participate in collaborative projects that align with minimalist values, such as community clean-ups or sustainability initiatives. These activities not only contribute to the greater good but also reinforce your minimalist practices. **Hint:** Ask yourself, "How can I contribute to my community in a way that reflects my minimalist values?" **Encouragement:** By connecting with others and contributing to your community, you create a network of support that helps sustain your minimalist lifestyle and spreads the benefits of simplicity to those around you.

Looking Forward with Minimalism

As you continue your minimalist journey, focus on setting future goals that reflect your values and aspirations. Embrace continuous growth and improvement, recognizing that minimalism is an ongoing process of refinement. Living with purpose means aligning your actions with your principles, and creating a life filled with joy, intention, and fulfillment. **Guidance:** Reflect on where you want your minimalist journey to take you in the future. **Encouragement:** Remember, minimalism is a journey, not a destination. Each step you take brings you closer to a life that resonates with your deepest values and desires. By setting thoughtful goals and embracing growth, you can continue to thrive, living a life that is not only simple but also richly fulfilling.

Conclusion

Recap of Everyday Minimalist Practices: To adapt minimalism into everyday use means making conscious and deliberate decisions that make existence more joyful. From being conscious about social life, choosing activities that reflect value systems and beliefs, packing lightly, or organizing basic events, every process enriches life in terms of clarity. Daily practice, being mindful, and making changes as needed are the ways to maintain the process of minimalism for years. Thus, by communicating with your community and planning for the future, you can make sure that your minimalism will stay interesting and fulfilling for you.

Encouragement for Ongoing Minimalism: As much as it may take a person a lot of hard work to maintain a minimalist lifestyle, the benefits are very fulfilling. In so doing, it becomes easier to live a simplified life as well as a life that falls in line with your beliefs or principles. Approach every one of the steps with pleasure because every tiny action equals a more mindful, meaningful life. Prompt: Most importantly, utilize the questions 'How can I make today simpler and better?' How can I ease the burden of the day?' It also helps to note that minimalism is a process that develops with the person. So, to stay on track with minimalism, stay with it and let the joy of a minimalistic life change you each day.

Inspiration for a Purposeful Life: Regarding the spirituality of minimalism it is a definition of better living free from unnecessary things that surround us and haven't anything to do with our core values and goals. You keep it simple and let it grow to the point where it can support what has real value, which is, first and foremost, people, the moments you spend together, and your development. This minimalist journey will help you lead a purposeful life of happiness by experiencing the liberty of having less and focusing on 'being'. Encouragement: It's very important to know that every change towards being simple is a step towards being more meaningful and fulfilling. Stay making it simple keep building a prosperous business and of course, have fun while at it.

Chapter 15: A New Beginning: Living Your Best Minimalist Life

Reflecting on Your Journey

Looking Back at the Transformation

Ending a minimalist journey also usually means that you get to sit back and realize how much your life has changed, for the better. In all probability, the candidate has undergone personal transformations in line with minimalism, including a better physical and mental state. This state of affairs has been made possible by your endeavors of designing a zone that is responsive to your authentic self, particularly the desire to obtain order and calmness. Remember that you can take time out at any point to properly soak up the victories and pleasures that have come from your major life change: doing so will keep them in your mind as everyday events that warrant appreciation and celebration. Admit the trials you have gone through—throwing away things you have accumulated, or changing certain routines for the better—and appreciate the spirit and stamina through which you have come thus far. Hint: Minimisation has of late transformed my life in many ways that I can list down below: **Encouragement:** Every move is a triumph of strength and resolve you have shown us and we commend you for them. Remember that all the hurdles you had to go over only serve to make the result all the sweeter.

Lessons Learned

The principles of minimalism can be instructive about what is important in this world. One that has been hailed by various philosophers is the notion of 'experience machines'. If you have made a specific switch that allows the focus of collecting items to change to the creation of experiences, you have probably discovered more happiness. The acceptance of change has been a theme that has run throughout your process, which has assisted you when it comes to change. In a minimalist way, you have discovered how to have your existence as a conscious and reflective experience where you make choices according to what is meaningful to you. **Prompt:** Think about how Minimalism has affected thinking of daily choices – what lessons have been most effective? **Encouragement:** Take these ideals and use them as advice for the coming years. They are the pathway to a life of meaning and purpose, providing the guideline for whatever you do in life.

Gratitude and Appreciation

Gratitude has likely played a key role in your minimalist lifestyle, helping you appreciate the simple joys of life. By incorporating gratitude into your daily routine, you've fostered a deeper sense of contentment and well-being. Simplicity brings with it a unique joy—a feeling of lightness and freedom that comes from living intentionally. As you reflect on your journey, take a moment to acknowledge the support you've received from family, friends, and your community. Their encouragement has been invaluable, helping you stay on course even when the journey seems challenging. Guidance: Consider keeping a gratitude journal to document the things you appreciate most in your minimalist life. Encouragement: Recognizing and celebrating the support around you reinforces the positive impact of your choices, strengthening your commitment to a life of simplicity and gratitude.

Inspirational Stories

Hearing about others' journeys can be incredibly inspiring as you reflect on your own. Many individuals have transformed their lives through minimalism, finding peace, joy, and purpose along the way. Communities, too, have been positively impacted, coming together to support sustainable practices and simpler living. This growing global movement toward minimalism and sustainability is a testament to the power of collective change. Hint: Share your own story with others—what inspired you to start, and what have been your greatest successes? Encouragement: By connecting with the broader minimalist community, you can draw inspiration from others' experiences and contribute to a worldwide shift toward intentional living. Remember, your story has the power to inspire change in others, creating a ripple effect that extends far beyond your immediate circle.

Embracing a Minimalist Future

Continual Growth and Learning

Remember that minimalism is not a final step or the end goal in the process, it's a lifelong process. Recognize the ability to continue learning and accept the new approaches that improve your minimalism as an important one. In this way, a minimalist lifestyle should be flexible, and be prepared to change the approach to achieving organization since life changes and it is necessary to improve some or all the habits. Minimalism does not have to be a one-time project, but a way of continuing education – the way to learn more about oneself and one's possibilities. **Guidance:** Do a check of what you have been doing in minimalism—where do you think you need to cut on your habits or enhance them? **Encouragement:** Continue to grow and develop as you do understand that every step which you take makes you closer to the values of minimalism and improves your existence.

Setting New Goals

When planning for the future it is useful to set new goals to reflect your new minimalist way of life. These aims may involve a process of increasing the extent of life's simplification, finding new interests, or enhancing the meaning of existence. Such longer-term goals help maintain the practicality of a minimalist life and that you are still receiving satisfaction from it. In particular, pay attention to the purposeful goals, in other words, the goals that have a meaningful direction to the genuinely desired improvement of the entire personality. **Prompt:** You can ask yourself: "What do I would like my minimalist path to be in the following five years?" **Support:** When embracing minimalism, a person purposefully maps out a way of life full of value and happiness, so they maintain a minimalist lifestyle, which brings only positive changes into their life.

Incorporating Minimalism in All Areas of Life

Minimalism is not just about cleaning up your spaces – it is about attacking the entire realm of your existence. For your work-related life, let us discuss how minimalism can make you a happier and more efficient employee. Keep focusing on the major aspects of health and the lifestyle regularities that help maintain the physical and psychological health of a person. Engage with people on a high level, and choose friends that you appreciate their company and share similar beliefs and principles with you. **Guidance:** Think over particular areas of your life that require the application of the concept of minimalism; how might your career, health, or relationships be enhanced thereby? **Encouragement:** Apparently, adopting minimalism in every aspect you is an effective way of achieving comprehensive change that enhances your life satisfaction.

Minimalist Legacy

Reflect upon what kind of environment you want to create for the following generations as you progress further. HL has found that talking to others about minimalist experiences motivates people to develop minimalist lifestyles. Engage in the positive changes in your community to make the world a better place to live. Focus on making the world a better place despite the desire to live a minimalist life because such a life improves one's life while giving back to society. **Hint:** Reflect on how your journey has been and how you can incorporate this into teaching new followers on the same. **Encouragement:** Minimalism is not about living with fewer things; its essence is about selecting what enables you to have a better life within the community and the whole world.

Celebrating Minimalist Wins

Recognizing Daily Wins

In the process of striving to achieve a minimalist lifestyle, it is crucially necessary to admire achievements that lead you to such objectives. Congratulations for clearing one drawer, and for deciding that you do not want to engage in the process of acquiring more things that will only fill up your space and occupy your time. All these small victories keep you on track and focused on a minimalist way of living and add to the sense of progression. Affirmative punishment such as rewarding yourself with something like a movie, or TV show, or even just congratulating yourself for the efforts made. **Hint:** All those tiny victories help you understand that you are gradually moving towards a less complicated and more profound existence. **Encouragement:** It's worth being happy about the cleanliness of a home or the acts of consciously selecting the right things in life or minimizing waste. It is crucial to remember that the point of minimalism is not having a perfect home – it is progression, so each achievement should be heralded even if it is small.

Sharing Your Success

Having a community of like-minded people, who can follow and be inspired by your minimalist accomplishments also helps in recovery and in creating a sense of belonging. To achieve this, offer to take before and after photos, share your own experience from the process, and tips that you have gained on-site, and on your pages in social nets. It helps interactively participate in minimalist online groups or meet people from offline, gain support, motivation, and advice from peers. Engage with those who are new to minimalism and try to guide them along the way and support them. **Guidance:** Try to concentrate on the changes for the better – whether big or slight- that one has undergone. **Encouragement:** It can help others kick off their minimalist process and cause a chain that will have a positive impact on other people's lives. Question yourself, whether your experiences might be useful to somebody else, and how, thus telling one's story gives camaraderie and ensures personal persistence.

Creating Minimalist Traditions

Coming up with minimalistic traditions is a great way of making your family bond even closer and stirring up the values that you hold dear. First of all, developing several family rituals does not necessarily mean that they must be associated with gift-giving: a dinner, a walk in the park, or a family game night. That is why the idea of restricting traditional presents and gifts and concentrating on the main idea of the holiday as people's togetherness is widely spread. Mini-birthday celebrations are yet another tradition: the last day of the year also marks the day of the yearly appraisals of your minimalist path and the goals set for the next year, as well as the day to look back on what you have achieved and moved forward. **Hint:** In other words, it doesn't always require a splendid tradition; it must be significant. **Encouragement:** In this way, by delegating in your life new traditions that are minimalistic, you stay in check, helping your family and friends embrace minimization and build long-lasting memories with them based on that.

Mindful Reflection

Regular reflection is essential for sustaining and deepening your minimalist practices. Schedule time to assess your progress, celebrate your successes, and identify areas where you can continue to improve. Mindful journaling is a powerful tool for reflection—use it to document your thoughts, track your journey, and set intentions for the future. Embrace continuous improvement, always seeking new ways to enhance your minimalist lifestyle. **Guidance:** Reflect on the positive changes minimalism has brought into your life, and consider what further steps you can take. **Encouragement:** Remember, minimalism is a journey of growth, and each reflection session is an opportunity to refine your approach and deepen your commitment. Ask yourself, "What have I learned from this journey, and how can I build on it?" Through regular reflection, you keep your minimalist journey aligned with your evolving goals and values.

Decluttering Motivation Tracker

Purpose: To keep track of your progress and maintain motivation throughout the decluttering process, this tracker allows you to record completed tasks, reflect on achievements, and set rewards for milestones.

Decluttering Progress Tracker

Area/Task	Date Started	Date Completed	Reflection	Check
Example: Kitchen Pantry	01/01/2024	01/02/2024	Feels organized; easier to find ingredients	[ ]
Living Room Shelves				[ ]
Bedroom Closet				[ ]
Home Office Desk				[ ]
Bathroom Cabinets				[ ]
Entryway and Coat Closet				[ ]

Motivation Milestones

Milestone	Reward	Check
Completed decluttering one room	Treat yourself to a favorite snack or meal	[ ]
Reached the halfway point in your decluttering process	Take a day off to relax or do something fun	[ ]
Finished decluttering your entire home	Plan a small celebration or buy something meaningful for your newly organized space	[ ]
Maintained a clutter-free home for one month	Reward yourself with a new book, movie, or experience	[ ]
Achieved all your decluttering goals	Consider a larger reward, such as a weekend getaway or special purchase	[ ]

Decluttering Motivation Tracker

Reflection and Motivation Prompts

Prompt	Reflection/Answer	Check
How do I feel now compared to when I started decluttering?		[ ]
What has been the most rewarding part of this process?		[ ]
What challenges did I face, and how did I overcome them?		[ ]
How has decluttering impacted my daily life and routines?		[ ]
What will I do to maintain my newly organized space?		[ ]

Daily/Weekly Motivation Tracker

Day/Week	Goal	Completed	Reflection	Check
Day 1	Clear kitchen counters of unnecessary items	[ ]	Feels more spacious and easier to cook	[ ]
Day 2	Organize bathroom cabinets	[ ]	Everything is now within easy reach	[ ]
Week 1	Declutter entire bedroom	[ ]	The bedroom is more peaceful and restful	[ ]
Week 2	Sort and organize the home office	[ ]	The work environment is more productive and focused	[ ]

Living a Life of Intentionality and Joy

Intentional Living

Intentional living is the state in which people make appropriate decisions that are consonant with their values and purposes. It may be about being conscious about what you purchase, or what you use, it is more of the quality and the need for something. All the hours in a day, the dollars in your pocket, and everything you let into your home should be purposeful. When you deliberately start designing your life, you end up with a life that is less complex but more meaningful. **Hint:** As they say: Before I do anything today, I must ask myself, 'Does this serve my values and my objectives?': **Motivation to Action:** Intentional living is not about giving up; it's about creating room for the important things. In other words, when you orient your actions towards your purpose, then you generate a life of significance and happiness, with no room for ornamentation. Of course, any act of intentionality takes you closer to a life that aligns with who you are.

Finding Joy in Minimalism

Minimalism calls for you to find happiness in little things and the little things in life. It is a concept of getting to a point whereby one is content with what they have and does not yearn for much more. It means that if you discard the unnecessary load and give up unnecessary desire, you will be able to achieve those things that will make you happy. These are the common activities that turn into the basic needs of a happy life, such as taking a cup of tea in the morning, going for a nature walk, spending time with family or friends, and so on. **Guidance:** Remember that the things that make you happy and give you quiet time are the riches of minimalism. **Encouragement:** Plunge into a life full of happiness and start loving each day as it is the chance to tune in to the essentials. So let me remind you, that joy is not in objects, it is in the moments, in what happens around and to us. You should ask yourself the question, 'How can I make a little happiness today?'

Building a Supportive Community

Surrounding yourself with people who understand and encourage the decision to embrace minimalism is liberating. Having people who have similar beliefs inspires others, and creates motivation and other chances to grow together in the community. Discuss what you know and what you have learned, and try to make the atmosphere productive that would adapt everyone to effectively learn and grow. Be it via web platforms; face-to-face close groups and association get-togethers or gatherings, such relationships ensure you remain disciplined and dedicated to the modern minimalist persistence. **Hint:** Hunt for people who conform to the kind of characteristics that will fit well in your recovery process. **Encouragement:** So, the journey to minimalism doesn't have to be done on your own. This way, you establish a community of support to help everyone grow and promote the process of development and improvement. Decide at the beginning of the day to commit to both participating and learning in the community.

Looking Forward

As you continue your minimalist journey, envision a future where simplicity enhances every aspect of your life. Embrace the endless possibilities that come with living a minimalist lifestyle—whether it's more time for passions, deeper relationships, or a greater sense of peace. Stay inspired and motivated to live your best minimalist life, filled with intentionality, joy, and purpose. **Guidance:** Regularly revisit your goals and aspirations, adjusting them as your journey evolves. **Encouragement:** The future is full of potential when you live with intention. Each day is an opportunity to deepen your commitment to minimalism and explore new ways to simplify and thrive. Remember, minimalism is a journey of continuous growth—embrace it fully, and let it lead you to a life of fulfillment and joy.

Conclusion

Final Reflections: Finally, when you are reflecting on the period of having a minimalistic life, you should be proud of the change you have become. All have been leading you towards attaining a life that is orderly, purposeful, and meaningful, eliminating every unnecessary hindrance. This journey has not only created a new environment for you but also changed the lens of how you perceive the world and priorities in this world. Guidance: Debate on the main points you have gained and altered from the movie. Encouragement: Understand that your journey is a track to the achievement and consequence of the purpose of living a joyful life. Honor what you have achieved so far, and anticipate the changes you are still to achieve.

Encouragement and Motivation: In fact, the essence of minimalism goes beyond just the lifestyle; it is a plebeian lifelong process. Motivation mastery: Remember and be energized by the gains you've made up to now and the possibility of getting even more of what you want. Keep trying to live simply until you acquire all the elements of the life you imagine and aspire to live. Prompt: As you go through your day, pose the question: "How can I keep making my life even more simple and meaningful today?" Motivation: Remember how far you've come and that alone should be inspiration enough to keep pushing on. Any progress that is made no matter how small should be celebrated on the way to the minimalist way of life.

Gratitude and Farewell: Thank you for joining me in this minimalist series. Your commitment to eliminating clutter from your life is truly inspiring. I trust that the wisdom and guidance provided in this book have helped you live with more purpose and happiness. As you continue on your journey, remember that you are not alone—there are others who share your beliefs and are there to support you. I'm grateful to have been a part of your journey, and I sincerely wish you many victories as you embrace a simple, purposeful, and satisfying life.

Printed in Great Britain
by Amazon